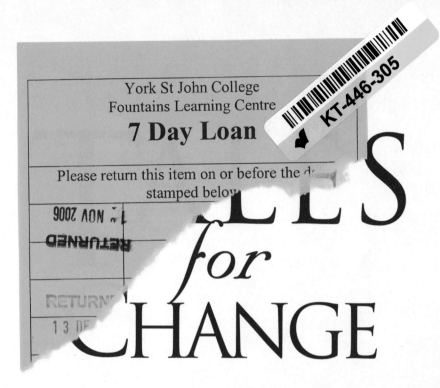

TALES for CHANGE

Using Storytelling to Develop People and Organizations

Margaret Parkin

**KOGAN
PAGE**

London and Sterling, VA

TALES *for* CHANGE

First published in Great Britain and the United States in 2004 by Kogan Page Limited

Apart from any fair dealing for the purposes of research or private study, or criticism or review, as permitted under the Copyright, Designs and Patents Act 1988, this publication may only be reproduced, stored or transmitted, in any form or by any means, with the prior permission in writing of the publishers, or in the case of reprographic reproduction in accordance with the terms and licences issued by the CLA. Enquiries concerning reproduction outside these terms should be sent to the publishers at the undermentioned addresses:

120 Pentonville Road
London N1 9JN
UK
www.kogan-page.co.uk

22883 Quicksilver Drive
Sterling VA 20166-2012
USA

© Margaret Parkin, 2004

The right of Margaret Parkin to be identified as the author of this work has been asserted by her in accordance with the Copyright, Designs and Patents Act 1988.

ISBN 0 7494 4106 2

British Library Cataloguing in Publication Data

A CIP record for this book is available from the British Library.

Library of Congress Cataloging-in-Publication Data

Parkin, Margaret.
  Tales for change : using storytelling to develop people and
organizations / Margaret Parkin.-- 1st ed.
    p. cm.
Includes bibliographical references and index.
  ISBN 0-7494-4106-2
  1. Communication in organizations. 2. Storytelling. 3.
Employees--Training of. 4. Organizational change. I. Title.
HD30.3.P366 2004
658.4'52--dc22
                        2003026739

Typeset by Jean Cussons Typesetting, Diss, Norfolk
Printed and bound in Great Britain by Biddles Ltd, King's Lynn
www.biddles.co.uk

Contents

Contents

Introduction

The link between storytelling and the concept of change and transition is as old as some of the stories themselves! The frog turns into the handsome prince, the ugly duckling becomes a beautiful swan and the poor cinder girl is transformed into a fairy princess – and gets the guy and a 'happy ever after' into the bargain!

Storytelling has always been a powerful tool for transition, whether used by nomadic tribes passing on cultural values through community storytelling, or by a shaman or pandit sharing wisdom through story to encourage learning. These original storytellers provided an invaluable service by helping people make sense of complex issues, by expressing the inexpressible, and offering comfort and support in difficult times. They were master communicators, who could ignite their listeners' imaginations through their use of language and visual imagery, and who developed immense levels of empathy and rapport with their listeners. Indeed, anthropologists tell us that, in many traditional tribes, it was an individual's skill as a storyteller that was a deciding factor in that person's being chosen as the chief, shaman or respected elder for the tribe.

Storytelling, although ancient, is by no means a dead art, and those who think of it as just the province of children are missing a huge resource. Any culture – whether it be a traditional tribe or a modern-day organization – uses storytelling, and just the same types of skills are required by storytellers today as were used thousands of years ago. Modern-day, organizational storytelling can sit just as comfortably in the boardroom or office, or emerge fresh-faced in the training room and conference centre. It can resonate in your ear when you are trying to convey a difficult concept, and tug at your sleeve during those awkward silences in presentations.

One of the great strengths of storytelling is in its flexibility – and there is a whole range of practical methods in which story and metaphor can be incorporated to help people and organizations through change and transition; for example:

- to communicate the future of the organization clearly and enthusiastically;
- to help people crystallize their own ideas for change;
- to add 'spice' and 'drama' to a presentation on forthcoming changes;
- as an aid to memorable learning;
- as part of an induction or orientation programme;
- as part of a one-to-one coaching session for coachees to reflect on and apply to their own situation;
- to encourage an individual in private contemplation or meditation;
- to encourage individuals to discuss and share their own fears or concerns about change;
- as part of a team briefing or brainstorming session during the change process;
- as pre-training work, for individuals to read, digest and then discuss their observations;
- as part of a training session, to aid discussion and reflection;
- to stimulate curiosity and interest in a 'change update' newsletter or e-mail.

Many people say to me, 'I would love to use more stories at work, but where do I find them?' Well, look no further! This book contains 50 stories, all of which have been specifically chosen to help you deal with the difficult and complex process of change. Some of the stories have been lent by other authors, some are my own creation, some were developed by participants during storytelling workshops and some have been re-told or adapted to address a particular aspect of change. As with my previous books, there is a 'moral' attached to the bottom of each story. In some situations you may feel it appropriate to disclose the suggested moral to your listener(s), but in others it may be more appropriate to allow them to reflect and formulate their own understanding. There is a danger of being over-prescriptive when sharing the meanings of stories; they always contain more than one meaning, as I have found on many occasions – and there's usually at least one that you never thought of!

There is also guidance in this book on how you might use the stories to promote reflection and meaningful discussion. Each story has its own accompanying matrix of 'reflections/trigger' questions, together with a blank section for listeners' comments or thoughts. You may feel quite confident just to use this matrix as a guide. On the other hand, you may prefer to photocopy this sheet and hand it out to the groups or individuals you are working with. The stories in the book are categorized into five aspects of change:

1. **Dealing with change.** The stories in this section help us to deal with the notions that we sometimes have no choice but to change; that change is inevitable and constant; that we may be able to change our behaviour, but not necessarily our inner nature; that we have to be prepared to take action ourselves to change; and that too much change can be as bad as not enough. We are told that our perceptions determine our view of change; that we sometimes need to be reminded of the constant need for change and innovation; and that we can disguise change by appearing to keep things the same.
2. **Being creative.** This section shows how we can use stories and metaphors to 're-frame' and 're-size' a problem and see it from a more positive perspective; how we can take control of our own creativity; and how to train in thinking 'impossible things'. The stories warn us that in being creative we need to look to the heavens – but still have our feet on the ground – and to understand that there is often an element of risk in a creative venture. We learn how creative thinking is limitless thinking, and that creativity is not necessarily linked to intelligence.
3. **Leaders and teams.** The stories here illustrate how sometimes the greatest wisdom is found in simplicity; how we teach people about leadership through our own actions; how leaders and teams can become too dependent on each other; and how reluctant leaders can still make good leaders. We learn how teams who are united can withstand greater attack than individuals; how we can be individuals within a team and still part of a bigger whole; and how all individuals have some inherent worth if they can find their niche. We are warned to consider the image we are creating in our own organization; to beware of the ripple power of stories; and to remain open to the opportunities for learning.
4. **Dealing with stress.** The stories in this section help us to identify our priorities in life, and warn us not to allow the problems of the past to carry on into the future. We consider when it is right to persist and when to give up; how to limit the effect of a negative past; and how to be satisfied with what we have and not worried about what we don't have. These stories tell us that too little stress can be as bad as too much; that sometimes 'going with the flow' can be better than putting up a fight; and that happiness is a state of mind that comes from within.
5. **Emotional intelligence.** This final and very important section in the management of change helps us to develop our own self-awareness and awareness of others; we can consider different perceptions of truth, and understand another person's 'map of the world'. The stories show us how to deal with conflict; how we need to put theory

into practice in order to develop our 'emotional competencies'; how to be careful of making wrong 'first impressions'; and to 'do as we would be done by'. We are finally reminded of the inherent power in storytelling to generate strong emotions.

No-one would underestimate the difficulties of trying to get people and organizations to change the way they do things, and it would be naïve to think that a quick chorus of Little Red Riding Hood would make people instantly receptive to new ideas! But my experience over the years has been that storytelling is a powerful, compelling and somewhat under-valued resource that can certainly help the journey along, and a resource that is well worth keeping up your sleeve, either for your own personal use or for those that you work with… and talking of sleeves, a very good story is tugging at mine right now, demanding to be told…

CHAPTER 1

Dealing with Change

'Absolutum, obsoletum' – if it works, it's out of date!

(Stafford Beer)

The stories in this section help us to deal with the notions that we sometimes have no choice but to change; that change is inevitable and constant; that we may be able to change our behaviour, but not necessarily our inner nature; that we have to be prepared to take action ourselves to change; and that too much change can be as bad as not enough. We are told that our perceptions determine our view of change; that we sometimes need to be reminded of the constant need for change and innovation; and that we can disguise change by appearing to keep things the same.

HOW STORIES CAN HELP IN DEALING WITH CHANGE

Look in any book on change management, and I will guarantee that at some point you will come across words like 'transition', 'journey', 'transformation', 'metamorphosis' and 'growth'. Although just hearing these words can generate excitement and anticipation, they can also give rise to apprehension and resistance. Many of us are anxious about change; it requires us to move from a place where we feel relatively comfortable and safe, towards a place with which we are completely unfamiliar. Indeed, it may be a place that hasn't even been invented yet! Change and transition is hard for us, because it requires us to let go of habit and routine, to question our own thinking, our own values, and maybe even the beliefs and principles by which we have lived our lives so far.

For there to be a transition to a new place, we first have to turn our back on the old, and for a while we find ourselves in what William Bridges, in his book *Managing Transitions*, calls an 'emotional wilderness'. It is being in this neutral zone, where we have lost sight of our old identity and have not yet discovered a new one, that can be the greatest cause of anxiety for some, and yet, if managed properly, it can also be a time of great creativity and resourcefulness:

> Often people from troubled organizations or outsiders who do not know much about the subject come up with the breakthrough answers... Lacking clear systems and signals, the neutral zone is a chaotic time, but this lack is also the source of its positive aspect
>
> (Bridges, 1999)

Metaphor is one tool that helps us to make sense out of this chaos, and to navigate our way through the neutral zone. People in an organization I worked with recently, which was going through this stage, were describing the period metaphorically to me as 'jogging along, going nowhere', 'running up against a brick wall', 'wading through mud' and 'no idea of our direction' – sadly, there are no prizes for guessing how happy this particular band of people were! Advice given by Gareth Morgan (1997), in his book on organizations and metaphors, is:

> The challenge facing modern managers is to become accomplished in the art of using metaphor – to find appropriate ways of seeing, understanding, and shaping the situations with which they have to deal.
>
> (Morgan, 1997)

William Bridges tells the story of a manufacturing plant on the inevitable point of closure, where the process was regularly described as 'being on a sinking ship' by workers – who naturally couldn't wait to jump off! The skill of the manager is to find a new, more constructive – and also acceptable – metaphor that will enable people to 're-frame' the situation, to see things in a different and more positive light and to stretch their imaginations. In this case, they managed to turn the 'sinking ship' into one embarking on its 'last voyage', thereby giving employees a more positive feeling of being at least able to 'reach port' and 'disembark' in a controlled way.

Stories, which are sometimes known as 'extended metaphors', have a great part to play in dealing with change – your own or someone else's – because of their own transitional nature. The stages of transition that an organization or individual may go through can very often be mirrored by the stages of a story. The basic structure of most stories – sometimes referred to as the 'Story Map' – follows this line of transition:

1. 'Once upon a time' – the status quo, where the story begins.
2. 'Then one day' – the characters encounter some problem or challenge.
3. 'Because of this' – the story changes direction to deal with the problem.
4. 'The climax' – the characters deal with the challenge.
5. 'The resolution' – the result of the action.
6. 'The moral' – the characters learn lessons as a result of their actions; their lives are changed.

We can see where an organization might take the same route:

Story Transition	Organizational Transition
1. 'Once upon a time…' The status quo – where the story begins and we meet the characters of the story.	1. The organization has been operating in the same way for some time.
2. 'Then one day…' The status quo is broken; the characters encounter a problem, conflict, discomfort or challenge.	2. Internal or external forces dictate the need for change. These forces may have been predictable – or completely unanticipated.
3. 'Because of this…' The characters effect a change of direction.	3. The organization may change its vision, its product, its people, its location, to respond to the challenge.
4. 'The climax…' The characters deal with the challenge, either successfully or unsuccessfully.	4. The organization plans, communicates and implements the changes and makes steps in its new direction.
5. 'The resolution…' The consequence of the action taken by the characters.	5. Periodic reviews are carried out to assess success or otherwise.

6. '… and the moral of the tale is…'	6. The organization, by periods of reflection, can learn valuable lessons.
7. The characters' lives are not the same.	7. Subsequent challenges are handled differently; individuals may have grown, although some may not have survived the change.

Even the shortest story can follow the same 'journey' format. In my second book, *Tales for Coaching* (2001), there is a humorous tale about two caterpillars who, whilst sitting together on a cabbage leaf, suddenly hear a swishing noise, and look up to see a beautiful butterfly flying overhead. The first caterpillar looks at the other, shakes his head and says, 'You'll never get me up in one of those things.' The tale itself is only four lines long, and yet, on the numerous occasions I have used it, has proved to be a powerful tool for illustrating the complexities of change – the resistance to the idea of transition, the inability to see oneself in another dimension and the inevitability of change are all contained within the metaphor.

Stories for change can be used to add passion to a presentation on the future of an organization, as part of a change management team briefing session, as discussion prompts in training sessions or for individual coaching or private contemplation. The stories in this section help with these particular aspects of change:

- Sometimes we have no choice but to change.
- Change is inevitable.
- We may be able to change our behaviour – but do we *really* change our inner nature?
- Sometimes we only move forward when there are no other options.
- We might say we want to change – but are we really prepared to take action ourselves?
- Socrates said 'Remember that there is nothing stable in human affairs; therefore avoid undue elation in prosperity, or undue depression in adversity.'
- Our perceptions determine whether change is good or bad.
- Too much change – particularly if random and unstructured – can be as bad as not enough.
- Large organizations need 'irritant individuals', like elephants need fleas to remind them of the need for change and innovation.
- You can disguise change by appearing to keep things the same.

1

INTRODUCTION

The inspiration for this story came from participants in a storytelling workshop I ran for Ardis Consulting, based in The Hague, the administrative capital of the Netherlands. The group came up with this metaphor to help address the problem of a young manager who was finding it difficult to motivate an older colleague to accept change.

THE TALE

The Old Bear and the Young Bear

Once upon a time, in a forest on a hill lived an old bear and a young bear. The young bear loved to play in the forest, to chase the squirrels and to bask in the sun. The old bear, on the other hand, liked nothing better than to spend most of his time sleeping in his favourite cave. One day, the young bear, lonely and looking for a playmate, ran into the cave and tried to persuade the old bear to wake up.

'Wake up, wake up, old bear,' he said. 'Please come and play with me in the forest. Come and chase the squirrels, and bask in the sun.'

'Go away, little bear, and let me sleep,' the old bear said. 'It's not yet time to get up.'

'But when will you get up?' asked the young bear, tugging at the other's furry back.

'Only when the spring has arrived,' said the old bear.

'But how will you know when spring has arrived?' asked his young companion.

'When the sun is high in the sky, and I can feel the gentle warm breeze on my fur,' replied the old bear. 'Then I'll know that spring is truly here.'

The young bear, desperate for a playmate, painted a huge sun on the roof of the cave where the old bear was sleeping and, using branches from the fir trees, wafted air in through the mouth of the cave.

'Wake up, wake up, old bear!' he said. 'See, the sun is shining and the breeze is blowing. The spring is here.'

But the old bear remained just where he was.

'Go away, little bear, and let me sleep. I know that you are trying to trick me. It's not yet time to get up.'

'But when *will* you get up?' asked the young bear anxiously.

'Only when I know that spring has arrived,' said the old bear.

'But how will you know when spring has arrived?' asked his young companion.

'When the birds are singing their special song,' said the old bear. 'Then I'll know that spring is truly here.'

The young bear ran into the forest and, as quickly as he could, laid a trail of breadcrumbs to the entrance of the cave that the birds could follow. And sure enough, before too long, a huge flock of birds were flapping and fluttering outside the cave, pecking at the food and singing loudly.

'Wake up, wake up, old bear!' said the young bear. 'Listen – the birds are singing for you. The spring is here.'

But the old bear remained just where he was.

'Go away, little bear, and let me sleep. I know that you are trying to trick me. It's not yet time to get up.'

'But when *will* you get up?' asked the young bear, growing in impatience.

'Only when I'm convinced that spring has truly arrived,' said the old bear.

The young bear left the cave and started to walk dejectedly towards the forest, but no sooner had he got outside than suddenly he heard in the distance the sound of men shouting, dogs barking and guns firing. He ran back to the cave in alarm.

'Please, *please* wake up, old bear!' he cried. 'Listen – the hunters are coming for us. We must leave our cave before they find us!'

With one great movement, the old bear raised himself up.

'Very well, little bear,' he said. 'I know that this is not a trick. Now I know that the spring *is* truly here.'

MORAL

Sometimes we have no choice but to change.

10

Reflections/ Trigger	Comments/ Thoughts
1. What change(s) are imminent for you and your organization?	
2. Who is represented by the young bear and the old bear?	
3. Will there be resistance to change in your organization? What form might it take?	
4. Who is represented by the 'hunters' in the tale, who may enforce the need for change?	
5. What will happen if you/others don't change?	

2

INTRODUCTION

This is a well-known traditional Buddhist story that speaks to all of us in some way. It can be tempting, if one is going through some sort of change that involves a feeling of sadness or loss, to feel that no-one else has experienced the same degree of suffering. This tale helps us to put those feelings into context.

THE TALE

The Mustard Seed

In a land far away lived a young woman called Kisagotami. She had only one son, whom she loved with all her heart. But the young boy fell sick and, despite all Kisagotami's efforts to save him, he tragically died. Distraught at her loss and unable to accept the child's death, she went to each of her friends, saying, 'Please save my child', but each of them said the same: 'The child is dead, Kisagotami. There is nothing now that can save him.'

Refusing to accept their words, she carried the child in her arms to the Buddha, and weeping said, 'Please save my child. Please give me a medicine that will cure him.'

Buddha with wisdom and compassion told Kisagotami that he would make a medicine for the child, but that he would require some special ingredients, amongst which was a handful of mustard seed.

'But', the Buddha added, 'you must get the mustard seed from a household where not one of the inhabitants has died – parent, child or servant.'

Kisagotami set off round the village, and went from house to house in the hope of finding such a mustard seed. And every person she spoke to gladly offered her the seed in the hope that it would save the child's life. But when she enquired whether anyone had died in the house, every single household had suffered such a loss – at the first house it was the husband, at the second a daughter, at the third an old grandmother. Not one household had escaped suffering.

Sadly, Kisagotami returned to the Buddha and, very gently laying her child's lifeless body on the ground, said to the Buddha, 'I understand now what you and others were trying to tell me.'

The Buddha with compassion said to Kisagotami, 'You thought that you were alone in your suffering. But such is the nature of life that no one can escape the suffering of impermanence.'

MORAL

Change is inevitable.

Reflections/ Trigger	*Comments/ Thoughts*
1. In way way can you relate the story to your own experience of change?	
2. What change have you/others found hard to accept?	
3. The story implies that change is inevitable – do you agree?	
4. Does anyone escape the 'suffering of impermanence'?	
5. How does it help to think of everything as 'impermanent'?	

3

INTRODUCTION

I'm very often amused when I visit supermarkets and other retail organizations where the staff sport badges saying things like 'happy to help', 'here to serve' etc when their whole demeanour and behaviour say the very opposite! Just sticking a badge on people does not necessarily change their beliefs. And without that change, it is unlikely that the behaviour will be sustained – as Aphrodite discovered in this next story (although not in a supermarket!).

THE TALE

The Cat and her Lover

Once there was a cat, who saw and fell in love with a handsome young man. She went to Aphrodite, the goddess of love, and begged her to change her into a woman, so that she might meet with the young man and make him her lover. Aphrodite, feeling sorry for the cat and her plight, agreed and transformed her into a beautiful young woman. Upon seeing the woman, the young man instantly fell in love with her and took her to be his bride.

The first night, whilst they were alone in their bedchamber, Aphrodite, who could not resist her own curiosity as to whether the cat's instincts had changed along with her appearance, let loose a mouse into the room. The young woman, completely forgetting where and who she was, instantly leapt off the bed and chased the mouse in order to eat it.

Aphrodite, disappointed in the young woman's behaviour, immediately changed her back to a cat.

MORAL

We may be able to change our behaviour – but do we really change our inner nature?

Reflections/ Trigger	Comments/ Thoughts
1. What do you understand as the meaning of the story?	
2. Who is represented by the cat in your organization?	
3. Has this person changed his or her inner nature – or just behaviour?	
4. What 'mouse test' could you set?	
5. Discuss how the story might have ended differently.	

4

INTRODUCTION

We have taken the expression 'burning the boats' into our everyday language. This is the story of Hernando Cortes, to whom the action is attributed. It is a powerful metaphor for helping people to tackle the notion of change boldly – and to realize that in some cases it is best if we don't look back…

THE TALE

Burning the Boats

Hernando Cortes was born in Spain in 1485. He left home at the age of 14 to study law at the University of Salamanca, but his ambition in life was to become a conquistador, or conqueror, as well as an explorer. In his twenties and thirties, he had many adventures around the seaports of Cadiz, Palos and Seville, and eventually joined forces with another explorer called Diego Velasquez. Together, their goal was to conquer the Aztec capital city of Tenochtitlan.

Cortes and his team of some 500 soldiers set off in the year 1519, and, having landed at a village that Cortes later named Veracruz, he soon realized that some of his men wanted to return to Cuba, rather than facing the journey ahead – they would have to navigate some 200 miles of jungle and swampland prior to attacking the fortress city itself, which was surrounded by water.

Expecting mutiny from his men, Cortes took the bold and unexpected step of ordering all their own boats to be burnt. With no way to retreat, the soldiers had just two options left – to fight or die. The expedition duly went on to fight the Aztecs and successfully conquer Tenochtitlan, which later became known as Mexico City.

MORAL

Sometimes we only move forward when there are no other options.

Reflections/ Trigger	*Comments/ Thoughts*
1. In what way can you relate the story to your own experience?	
2. Who is represented by Cortes and his team in your organization?	
3. What is the expedition you/others are on? What is the goal at the end of the journey?	
4. How could you 'burn your boats' to ensure there is no going back?	
5. What would be the impact of this bold move?	

5

INTRODUCTION

Someone told me this story in a smoky hotel bar somewhere – so long ago, I'm afraid I've forgotten who and the point that the person was making! But I like to use it when groups are engaged in their favourite game of 'change involves everybody else but me...' In other words, it seems easier to get others to take action rather than taking action yourself!

THE TALE

The Cigarette Story

A man, desperate to give up smoking, read an advertisement in the local newspaper, which read:

> WANT TO MAKE POSITIVE CHANGES IN YOUR LIFE?
> SEND £5 FOR AN INSTANT AND GUARANTEED CURE FOR SMOKING.

Intrigued and thinking that, having tried everything else, he had nothing much to lose, he duly sent off his money and waited for the miracle cure to arrive on his doorstep.

Sure enough, a few days later, a small envelope arrived and, although disappointed at its size, the man eagerly tore it open. Inside was a small card on which were the words:

> INSTANT AND GUARANTEED CURE FOR SMOKING
>
> 1. DON'T BUY ANY CIGARETTES.
> 2. DON'T BORROW ANY FROM A FRIEND.

MORAL

We might say we want to change – but are we really prepared to take action ourselves?

Reflections/ Trigger	*Comments/ Thoughts*
1. Should the man have asked for his £5 back?!	
2. What change are you/others trying to make?	
3. What action do you need to take?	
4. The story implies that we have to take responsibility for our own actions and not rely on others. Do you agree?	
5. How could you encourage others to take more responsibility for themselves?	

6

INTRODUCTION

I told this story just the other day to a department manager who had for some time been suffering from stress, and now jubilantly pronounced herself as 'over it'. I was concerned that her newly acquired and almost euphoric state of 'high' might prove in time to be just as undesirable as the 'lows'. I told her this tale, not wanting to burst the bubble or dampen her enthusiasm, but in the hope that she might achieve more balance in her life.

THE TALE

King Solomon's Ring

King Solomon was the King of Israel in the 10th century BC and was famed for his wisdom and for the magnificence of some of his temples and cities. He once asked his councillors to design and make him a ring with a special inscription. He told them, 'I want the words to make me change my mood – whether it be from sorrow to joy, or joy to sorrow.'

The councillors wrestled with the task that Solomon had set them for a long time, but eventually presented him with the ring on which were inscribed the words: 'This too shall pass'.

MORAL

Socrates said, 'Remember that there is nothing stable in human affairs; therefore avoid undue elation in prosperity, or undue depression in adversity.'

Reflections/ Trigger	*Comments/ Thoughts*
1. How do you react to hearing the words 'This too shall pass'?	
2. Are you guilty of 'undue elation' or 'undue depression', as Socrates remarked?	
3. Is everything we know subject to change?	
4. Discuss why you think King Solomon asked for this inscription.	
5. How could you change your own or others' moods? Is this possible?	

7

INTRODUCTION

You might think that this story brings into question the ethics of some psychological experiments, but nevertheless it is an interesting one to illustrate the destructive effects of badly introduced change on animals – and that of course includes us!

THE TALE

Rats in the Maze

Some years ago, a professor from Michigan University performed a number of experiments on rats to investigate the causes of stress and neurosis. The rats were trained to jump at one of two doors in a maze. If they jumped towards the left, the door would open and they would receive a pellet of food. The door on the right of the maze would remain shut and they would simply receive a bruised nose for their pains. Naturally, the rats (being intelligent animals) quickly learnt to jump towards the left.

After some time, when the rats had become used to this regime, the investigators decided to change the rules, and switched the doors so that the left door then produced nothing, whereas the right door was the one that issued the reward. Although, understandably, a little peeved at first, the rats soon adjusted to the change and started habitually jumping towards the right door in order to receive the food.

Then the researchers decided to 'up the level' of the experiment and make the rules even more complex. So some days, when the rats were exposed to the maze, they had to jump to the right and some days they had to jump to the left. The choice was purely random, and the rats would never know, on any given day, which door would produce the food. This final random change proved too much for the rats; they quickly showed signs of major distress, to the extent that they eventually refused to jump at all, but sat comatose in the middle of the maze.

MORAL

Too much change – particularly if random and unstructured – can be as bad as not enough.

Reflections/ Trigger	*Comments/ Thoughts*
1. How is change introduced in your organization – is it done randomly or is there a logical structure to it?	
2. How do people generally react to change in your organization?	
3. How might people in your organization be trained to adapt to change?	
4. What represents the pellet of food, ie the incentive for making the change?	
5. Has there been too much change too quickly in your organization? How would you know?	

8

INTRODUCTION

It's amazing how two people can view what appears to be exactly the same situation in completely different ways – and, of course, both views are 'right' in terms of each person's perception. This is a traditional tale that has appeared in many guises over the years. It encourages us to examine our own behaviour before being too critical of other people's.

THE TALE

Perception and Reality

Two young men had both worked for the same company for a long time, and were shocked when, without a great deal of warning, the company closed down and they found themselves unemployed. Both went on the search for work.

The first man was very concerned. He hated the idea of change, having to learn new things and meet new people – but he reminded himself that he had no choice if he wanted to make some money. The second man was more philosophical and thought of the change as an opportunity to move on. Unbeknown to each other, both men went for an interview for a position in the same organization. The company was very similar to the one that they were leaving.

The first man sat nervously through his interview, and towards the end was asked if he had any questions.

'Yes,' he said, 'can you tell me what the people in this company are like?'

The interviewer, a wise old man who was one of the founders of the company, leant forward across the table and replied, 'Before I answer your question, first tell me about the place you have just left. What were the people like there?'

'Not very nice at all, I'm afraid,' replied the young man, with some feeling. 'They were very difficult people, quarrelsome and stubborn.'

'Then I'm afraid to tell you that you will find them just the same here,' said the old man.

The next day, the second man arrived for his interview, and he was also asked if he had any questions.

'Oh, yes,' he said, cheerily, 'can you tell me what the people in this company are like?'

Again, the old man replied, 'First tell me about the place you have just left. What were the people like there?'

'Oh, they were wonderful,' the young man enthused. 'They were warm and welcoming, courteous and kind; I was so sorry to leave.'

The old man said with a smile, 'In that case, I'm pleased to tell you that you will find them just the same here.'

MORAL

Behaviour breeds behaviour.

Reflections/ Trigger	Comments/ Thoughts
1. How can you relate the story to your own experience?	
2. Do you agree with the notion that 'behaviour breeds behaviour'?	
3. How could you encourage others to examine themselves more than criticizing others?	
4. What problems might be associated with the behaviour of the first man?	
5. How might this story relate to your/others' handling of people in your organization?	

9

INTRODUCTION

Charles Handy, as well as a brilliant observer of life in organizations, is also a skilful storyteller. His latest book, The Elephant and the Flea *(2002), is a colourful metaphor in itself, that draws our attention to the need for what he calls 'irritant individuals' to remind, particularly some of the large conglomerates, of the constant need for change and innovation.*

THE TALE

The Need for Change

The *Encyclopaedia Britannica* management remained convinced that people would always want their collection of handsomely bound volumes, costing several thousand pounds, displayed on shelves in their living rooms. They sat and watched their revenues fall as first the *Grolier Encyclopaedia* was published on CD ROM for $385 and then, in 1993, Microsoft's Encarta, which also included multimedia, became available for $100. Within a year, *Britannica* had collapsed and the business had been sold. It has since been resurrected by its new owners as a free online information service financed by ads, but the brand has been damaged. All this is obvious in hindsight or to outside observers, but hindsight is only of use to the writers of the obituaries.

(Extract from *The Elephant and the Flea* by Charles Handy published by Hutchinson. Used by permission of The Random House Group Limited.)

MORAL

Elephants need fleas scratching their skin to help them see the obvious before it is too late.

Reflections/ Trigger	*Comments/ Thoughts*
1. Do you agree with Handy's observations?	
2. Is your organization, or one you know, an 'elephant'? In what way?	
3. Discuss other examples of well-known 'elephant' organizations!	
4. Who or what might represent the 'flea' for you or other organizations?	
5. Could you become a 'flea' for someone else?!	

10

INTRODUCTION

Recently, at Training Options, we had to change to using a different awarding body for one of our management qualifications. Initially, the new regime seemed so complex, bureaucratic and completely different to what I was used to that I was on the point of having a major tantrum – not a sight to behold! It was only when a colleague pointed out to me the similarities between the new regime and what we were currently doing that I started to make sense of it. This extract from Machiavelli (1469–1527) illustrates the principle he might have been using.

THE TALE

Keep Things the Same

He who desires or attempts to reform the government of a state, and wishes to have it accepted, must at least retain the semblance of the old forms; so that it may seem to the people that there has been no change in the institutions, even though in fact they are entirely different from the old ones. For the great majority of mankind are satisfied with appearances, as though they were realities.

MORAL

Disguise change by appearing to keep things the same.

Reflections/ Trigger	*Comments/ Thoughts*
1. In what way can you follow Machiavelli's advice?	
2. What situations are you trying to change at present in your organization?	
3. Do people tend to look for 'the same' or 'different' during periods of change?	
4. How can you identify similarities between the old regime and the new?	
5. How could you convince others of the similarities?	

CHAPTER 2

Being Creative

'Nothing is more dangerous than an idea when it is the only one we have.'

(Emile Chartier)

This section shows how we can use stories and metaphors to 're-frame' and 're-size' a problem and see it from a more positive perspective; how we can take control of our own creativity; and how to train in thinking 'impossible things'. The stories warn us that in being creative we need to look to the heavens – but still have our feet on the ground, and to understand that there is often an element of risk in a creative venture. We learn how creative thinking is limitless thinking, and that creativity is not necessarily linked to intelligence.

HOW STORIES CAN HELP IN BEING CREATIVE

Those of you who, like me, grew up with Winnie-the-Pooh may remember how his creator, A A Milne, one of our greatest storytellers, introduces his hero:

> Here is Edward Bear, coming downstairs now, bump, bump, bump, on the back of his head, behind Christopher Robin. It is, as far as he knows, the only way of coming downstairs, but sometimes he feels that there really is another way, if only he could stop bumping for a moment and think of it.

People and organizations cannot hope to make progress without imagining creative solutions, and one of the functions of story and metaphor in this context is to allow us time to stop 'bumping downstairs' for a moment, long enough to sit and ponder if there really *is* another way.

During periods of change, it is natural for individuals to become tense and anxious – and when we're tense, our levels of creativity can plummet to zero! The findings of such researchers as Hart (1975), Lozanov (1978) and O'Keefe and Nadel (1978) suggest that the brain actually operates differently when any type of threat is perceived – either physical or emotional. In such circumstances, the brain uses less of the sophisticated creative thinking activity that comes from the neocortex, and resorts instead to using basic survival-type thinking that comes from the reptilian brainstem area. And yet, paradoxically, this is the very time when we need to muster all the creative thought we can; we can't realistically expect to tackle current problems using solutions that were applicable ten, five or even just two years ago.

Work carried out by Mitroff and Kilman in 1995 advocates using storytelling as a creative approach to organizational problem solving. Incorporating what they term 'epic myths', they found that, by first sharing stories about ideal organizations, individuals were more receptive to then discussing their own and would think more creatively about how ideas from the one might be introduced into the other. My own experience has been similar: the traditional story 'The Enormous Turnip', from my first book, *Tales for Trainers* (1998), is a useful example of how an unlikely team (made up of a man, woman, girl, dog, cat and mouse) can still work together collaboratively to achieve a common goal – ie pulling up a turnip! Sharing and discussing this fictitious (and unlikely) story with a group seems to enable them to suspend their analytical, left-brain thinking about themselves long enough to identify the principles that go to make an effective team, which can later be applied, more creatively, to their own situation. Steven Denning, now a well-known advocate of using what he calls 'springboard' stories in organizations, says, 'Storytelling doesn't replace analytical thinking. It supplements it by enabling us to imagine new perspectives and new worlds, and is ideally suited to communicating change and stimulating innovation' (2001).

It is the power of story to engender empathy with the protagonist that draws the listener into the tale and engages the conscious analytical mind, leaving the unconscious to work on more creative solutions, ie the 'springboard effect'. And, as some of the examples in this book illustrate, open-ended stories, where a number of solutions are possible, and 'dilemma tales', which very often pose a moral quandary to which there is no definitive answer, also give the listener a perceived power in determining a resolution.

On a personal level, creativity works by our deriving new meaning from connections and associations, or what Tony Buzan (1993), creator of the MindMap system, calls 'radiant thinking'. Stories and metaphors can help us to build on this process by encouraging us to use our brains in a different, sometimes unconventional way, and connecting with seemingly unconnected things. For example, if I were to ask you to describe the nature of your job, you would no doubt give me a very sensible answer, quoting huge chunks from your job description, but if I were then to ask you to consider how your job was similar to a banana, say, or an item of clothing or an act in the circus, then (having backed away from me quickly!) you would start to make completely new neuronal connections in your brain – in other words, you would boldly go to those areas of your brain where you had never gone before!

Similarly, the original storytellers used their brains in a very different way to what must have been the norm at the time. Firstly, in order to make sense of and remember the information they had to pass on, they developed their own personal methods of visualization, creating vivid and fantastic images in their mind and linking or 'pegging' the information on to it. Secondly, they used similar techniques to get their message across to their listeners, weaving fact and fiction together skilfully, to create a story that generated interest and curiosity and aroused emotion in the listener. Storytelling is a sophisticated mental process that draws together the logical, verbal thinking that we associate with the left brain together with visual and emotional thinking that is more typical of the right brain.

The link between stories, metaphors and creative people has been well documented throughout history – Einstein worked on his theory of relativity by daydreaming and imagining himself riding on a beam of light to the end of the universe, and Alexander Graham Bell created the telephone after drawing an analogy with the workings of the human ear. The Greek philosopher Heraclitus, who described change as a river where the waters were continually flowing, was probably one of the first to use the concept around 500 BC. Charles Handy, in 2002, using the metaphor of the 'elephant and the flea' to explain why large organizations need irritant individuals to stimulate innovation, shows that the process is still going strong!

But what of the rest of us? Rosabeth Moss Kanter (2002) warns that, as a leader in an organization, it is relatively easy to allocate resources for new product development, or re-organize a unit, but you cannot *order* people to use their imaginations. Many people try to avoid the issue by describing themselves as inherently 'un-creative', as though creativity were a rare gift bestowed only on artists, musicians and the occasional hairdresser, and yet Boden (1996) says

> Creativity draws crucially on our ordinary abilities. Noticing, remembering, seeing, speaking, hearing, understanding language and recognising analogies – all these talents of Everyman are important.
>
> (Boden, 1996)

Stories, metaphors and story-based activities can be wonderful triggers to bring out these 'ordinary abilities' of people and organizations. They can be used as part of a strategic planning, brainstorming or MindMapping session, they can be used to unpick a problem and offer a parallel view and they can encourage people to see that there is not just one solution to a problem but very often a great many. In addition, stories and metaphors can help us to express the inexpressible. Just like Einstein and Heraclitus before us, we may find it impossible to articulate our thoughts about an idea or concept to others, but using story and metaphor can make it easier – and in some cases safer and more acceptable!

The stories in this section deal with these aspects of creativity and change:

● Stand back and look for the bigger, more positive side of the picture.
● We need to empower people in the organization to take control over their own creative thinking.
● There is always more than one way of tackling a problem.
● Don't condemn or ridicule people in your organization who may be thinking creatively.
● You can believe impossible things – if you believe you can!
● Look to the heavens for creative inspiration – but have your feet on the ground.
● All adventures involve risk – but staying still can involve more risk.
● Most of us limit our creative viewpoint. Aim for the moon...
● Creativity doesn't always depend on education or intelligence.
● Beware of aiming too high in your creative thinking – or too low.

11

INTRODUCTION

Some of you may remember, from my second book, the story of my visits to a Buddhist centre in the North of England. Since then, I have heard many words of wisdom there – not all of it's sunk in, I have to say – and not all of it has come from the expected source! This is a nice (true) story that can help people who are 'stuck' with a particular problem, to see it from a broader perspective.

THE TALE

The Monk's Room

What is now known as the Madhyamaka Buddhist centre was once a privately owned, and in its day probably very opulent, Georgian mansion, set in 40 acres of green fields, lakes and woodland.

It is now a thriving and joyful community of Buddhist practitioners – amongst them a mixture of monks, nuns and laypeople – and is well known as a highly successful teaching centre, running residential and day courses throughout the year, for people of all sorts from all over the world.

One of the teachers at the centre is a young monk called Kelsang Pandita. On one of my first visits there, we started chatting and, never having met a Buddhist monk 'up close and personal' before and ever the nosy inquisitor, I was dying to ask him what life was like for a young man like himself, who had made the decision to dedicate the rest of his life to spiritual development and the quest for enlightenment.

'How do you live? What possessions do you have? How do spend your day? Are a modern-day monk's living quarters *really* like a cell?' I fired questions curiously.

He laughed good-humouredly and, in response to my last question, said,

'Well, come and have a look!' and took me off into the bowels of the building. The monk's room was predictably tiny and, it has to be said, pretty spartan, the only real decoration being a shrine set up against one wall and a whole heap of scholarly books on a shelf in the corner.

'Well, it's very... uhhh...' My voice trailed into silence as I looked around the room, for once feeling lost for words. He laughed again when he saw my face.

37

'Don't worry,' he said. 'My mother's reaction was just the same. She thinks prisoners get a better deal. But then,' he added cheerily, 'I'm very lucky. How many other people can say they live in a mansion?'

MORAL

Always look for the bigger, more positive side of the picture.

Reflections/ Trigger	*Comments/ Thoughts*
1. How do you relate to the story?	
2. Are you/others taking an insular view of a particular situation?	
3. In what way might you see the bigger, more positive picture?	
4. What is represented by 'the mansion' that you might be living in?	
5. Imagine taking a step back from a situation that is troubling you – what does it look like from this new position?	

12

INTRODUCTION

I first heard this story told by Ben Haggarty, a very skilful storyteller, at a meeting of the Society for Storytelling in the UK. I have found it particularly powerful for promoting discussion on such concepts as the effect of disempowerment on creativity, passive and active attitudes to learning and taking responsibility for your own actions.

THE TALE

The Old Man in the Market Place

Many years ago, in a land far away, there was an old man, making his way slowly through the market place. Just as he was about to leave, a young man suddenly stepped out from behind a building and stood in front of him, barring his way.

Alarmed, the old man said, 'Please let me pass.'

But the young man smiled and shook his head. 'I want something from you, old man,' he said.

'Very well,' said the old man. And with a flourish he pointed his finger at a chicken that was running across the road in front of them. Immediately the chicken stopped running and, before their eyes, turned into solid gold. The old man picked it up and gave it to the young man, saying, 'Now, will you let me pass?'

The young man took the golden chicken, but continued to smile and shake his head. 'I want more from you, old man,' he said.

'Very well,' said the old man, and again with a flourish he pointed his finger, this time at a dog, who was just in the middle of relieving himself against a wall. Once again, the dog froze and immediately turned into a solid gold statue (cocked leg and all). The old man picked up the dog and gave it to the young man, saying, 'There you are. Now will you let me pass?'

The young man took the dog, but still shook his head, saying, 'It's not enough. I want more from you, old man.'

'Very well,' said the old man, and again he pointed his finger, this time at a house on the edge of the market place. As the two of them watched, brick by brick the house too was transformed into solid, gleaming gold that dazzled them in the sunshine. 'There you are,' said the old man, pointing at the house. 'Now, *surely* you will let me pass.'

But the young man remained standing just where he was in front of the old man. 'It's still not enough,' he said.

Exasperated, the old man cried, 'But what else can I give you?'

The young man stepped closer and, taking hold of the other's hand, replied, 'I want... the finger.'

MORAL

Give a man a fish and you feed him for a day. Teach a man to fish and you feed him for a lifetime.

Reflections/ Trigger	*Comments/ Thoughts*
1. What do you understand as the meaning of the story?	
2. Who is represented by the old man and the young man in your organization?	
3. What power/knowledge/skills exist in your organization that might be given to someone else?	
4. Are some people in your organization expecting 'gifts' of knowledge?	
5. The young man wanted the power to create his own gold. How could you empower people in your organization?	

13

INTRODUCTION

I can't profess to being a particular lover of spiders, but I do remember, from my childhood, being a great fan of Anansi, an audacious and remarkably well-travelled arthropod (he turns up in Africa, the West Indies and Brazil!) who, through his own cunning and sometimes sheer arrogance, always seemed to get the better of his adversary. Anansi is one of a group of 'trickster' characters in storytelling, including Coyote, Brer Rabbit and Nasrudin, all of whom can teach us a thing or two about creative thinking!

THE TALE

Anansi Tricks the Snake

Many of you will have heard of the Anansi stories, which take their name from the cunning and wily spider who always seemed to get the better of his colleagues in the jungles of Africa many years ago – but what you might not know is how the stories came to be dedicated to him in the first place...

Long ago, all the animals knew and accepted that the Tiger, who proclaimed himself King of the forest, was the strongest and most powerful of them all, and that Anansi the Spider was the weakest and most feeble of them all. One day, the two creatures met, and Anansi, having bowed very low to greet the Tiger, said, 'I have a favour to ask of you, my King.'

'A favour?' the Tiger replied in a bemused voice. 'And what might that be, little Spider?'

'Well,' said Anansi, 'everyone knows that you are the strongest of all the animals and everyone knows your name – we have Tiger stripes and Tiger moths and Tiger lilies – but nobody has heard of me. No-one talks about Anansi.'

'Well,' said the Tiger, 'what exactly would you like to bear your name, Anansi?'

'The stories we tell,' said Anansi, nodding enthusiastically, 'the stories of Brer Rabbit and Brer Fox and all the other animals. I'd really like those to be known as "Anansi Tales".'

'Very well,' said the Tiger, although he secretly thought that 'Tiger Tales' had a much better ring to it, 'on one condition.' And, thinking of the hardest task he could, he said to the Spider, 'You know the big snake who

43

lives down by the river? Well, I would like you to bring me Brer Snake as a captive – but you must make sure that he's alive. Is it a deal?'

Anansi, at first rather apprehensively, but then remembering how much he wanted those stories, agreed to the challenge. After leaving the Tiger, he sat and thought about it and thought about it, and eventually came up with a plan.

The first day, he laid a trap for the Snake. He took a long piece of vine and tied a noose in it. Then, hiding the vine in the grass, he spread some of Snake's favourite berries all around the area – and then lay in wait. Sure enough, Brer Snake came along and, seeing the berries, crawled towards them and started to eat. Anansi pulled the vine to tighten the noose, but Snake was too heavy for him and he slid away unharmed.

Undaunted, on the second day Anansi dug a deep hole in the ground and smeared grease all over the sides. At the bottom of the hole, he put some of Snake's favourite bananas. Then he hid by the side of the road – and lay in wait. Sure enough, eventually Brer Snake came along and, seeing the bananas at the bottom of the hole, he first anchored himself safely, with his tail tied round the trunk of a tree, then reached down into the hole, ate the bananas, then carefully pulled himself out of the hole by his tail and again, much to Anansi's disappointment, slid away.

Anansi was beginning to think that this challenge was too great for him, but then, on the next day, he came across Brer Snake in the forest clearing.

'Anansi,' said the Snake, 'I know you have been trying to catch me all week, and you've failed. What should stop me from killing you on the spot, right now?'

'Well, you've found me out,' admitted the Spider. 'You're much too clever for me.' And then he added slyly, 'Yes... I was trying to catch you... but just to settle a bet that you are the *longest creature in the world*, longer than the Tiger's tail, longer than an elephant's trunk and *certainly* longer than that bamboo tree over there.'

The Snake turned and looked with disdain. 'Of course I'm longer than that bamboo tree,' he proclaimed. 'Why, I'm the longest creature in the whole world.'

'That's what I told them,' said the cunning Anansi. 'And yet, I have to admit that that bamboo tree does look pretty long – but, of course, it's difficult to tell from over there.'

'Well, let's bring it over here!' cried the Snake defiantly. 'Cut it down and lay it down beside me. Then you can convince yourself that I am the longer.'

Anansi did as the Snake requested and laid the bamboo tree next to him.

'Forgive me,' said the Spider, 'for I am small and foolish, but how will I know that when I run to the top of the tree you don't wriggle up to the top, and when I run to the bottom of the tree you don't just slide down again?'

'Well, tie my tail to the tree then,' said the Snake confidently, 'if you're not convinced. Then you'll know I'm telling the truth.'

Anansi did as the Snake told him, and tied the Snake's tail to the bottom of the bamboo tree. Then he ran down to the other end.

'Stretch yourself, Brer Snake!' he cried. 'Stretch as far as you can, and we will see who is the longer.'

Snake stretched as hard as he could and Anansi tied his middle to the bamboo.

'I'm afraid it's still not conclusive,' said the Spider. 'Take a rest, Snake, and then stretch again. Give it all you've got – close your eyes and *concentrate!*'

The vain and stupid Snake did as Anansi told him and, while he was stretching with all his might, with his eyes screwed shut, Anansi quickly tied his head to the bamboo. With the Snake now securely fastened to the tree, Anansi quickly got hold of his tail and towed him back to the waiting (and rather disappointed) Tiger.

And from that day on, the Tiger agreed that all the stories from the jungle should be called 'Anansi Stories'.

MORAL

There is more than one way to catch a snake!

Reflections/ Trigger	*Comments/ Thoughts*
1. What problem are you/others facing that requires a creative approach?	
2. What incentive do you/others have to achieve the goal?	
3. Was the fact that Anansi was much smaller and weaker than the Snake a problem to him?	
4. Sometimes creativity involves cheek! How could you be more audacious in your thinking?	
5. What other methods might Anansi have employed to catch the Snake?	

14

INTRODUCTION

I was recently invited to be a speaker for a conference held at Heriot-Watt University in Edinburgh and it reminded me of how, as a child, I had a bit of a 'thing' for James Watt. I think I must have been going through my 'inventor' period at the time! (It didn't last!) Anyway, I love this account of his childhood dreaming – a cautionary tale for all would-be parents of inventors…

THE TALE

James Watt's Story

James Watt, now hailed as the creator of the steam engine and one of the world's greatest inventors, was born in Greenock in Scotland on 19 January 1736.

His fond mother, having lost several of her children born previously, was intensely solicitous in her care of James, who was so delicate that regular attendance at school was impossible. The greater part of his school years he was confined for most of the time to his room. He was rated as a backward scholar at school, and his education was considered very much neglected. The following two stories of Watt's childhood proclaim the coming man.

In the first, a friend, looking at the child of six, said to his father, 'You ought to send your boy to a public school and not allow him to trifle away his time at home.'

'Look how he's occupied before you condemn him,' said the father.

James was trying to solve a problem in geometry. His mother had taught him drawing and with this he was captivated. A few toys were given him, which were constantly in use. Often he took them to pieces and, out of the parts, sometimes constructed new ones, a source of great delight. In this way he employed and amused himself in the many long days during which he was confined to the house by ill health.

The second story of James as a child comes from the journal of a Mrs Campbell, written in 1798.

James was sitting one evening with his aunt, Mrs Muirhead, at the tea table, when she said, 'James Watt, I never saw such an idle boy! Take a book or employ yourself usefully; for the last hour you have not spoken one word, but taken off the lid of that kettle and put it on again, holding now a cup and now a silver spoon, over the steam, watching how it rises from the spout and catching and connecting the drops of hot water it falls into. Are you not ashamed of spending your time in this way?'

(Extract from *Biography of James Watt* by Andrew Carnegie
published by Doubleday, Page & Co.)

MORAL

In the words of James Watt's father – look at how people are occupied before you condemn them.

Reflections/ Trigger	Comments/ Thoughts
1. All change involves some element of creativity – do you agree?	
2. Is there someone who might be a future 'James Watt' in your organization?	
3. Are people 'condemned' for appearing idle in your organization, or encouraged to think?	
4. What behaviour might be seen as 'idle' rather than potentially creative?	
5. How might creative thinking be better nurtured and encouraged in your organization?	

15

INTRODUCTION

Where would we be without Lewis Carroll's Alice books for creative inspiration? Their timeless nonsense seems to make more sense as you get older! This very well-known excerpt from Through the Looking Glass, *written in 1871, can be used to promote positive thinking and the power of creative imagination.*

THE TALE

Alice Meets the Queen

'Oh, don't go on like that!' cried the poor Queen, wringing her hands in despair. 'Consider what a great girl you are. Consider what a long way you've come today. Consider what o'clock it is. Consider anything, only don't cry!'

Alice could not help laughing at this, even in the midst of her tears. 'Can *you* keep from crying by considering things?' she asked.

'That's the way it's done,' the Queen said with great decision: 'nobody can do two things at once, you know. Let's consider your age to begin with – how old are you?'

'I'm seven and a half exactly.'

'You needn't say "exactually",' the Queen remarked. 'I can believe it without that. Now I'll give you something to believe. I'm just one hundred and one, five months and a day.'

'I can't believe *that* !' said Alice.

'Can't you?' the Queen said in a pitying tone. 'Try again: draw a long breath, and shut your eyes.'

Alice laughed. 'There's no use trying,' she said: 'one *can't* believe impossible things.'

'I daresay you haven't had much practice,' said the Queen. 'When I was your age, I always did it for half-an-hour a day. Why, sometimes I've believed as many as six impossible things before breakfast...'

(Extract from *Through The Looking Glass* by Lewis Carroll.)

MORAL

You can believe impossible things – if you believe you can!

Reflections/ Trigger	*Comments/ Thoughts*
1. Do you agree with the Queen's suggestion that you can 'keep from crying by considering things'? Have you tried it?	
2. Discuss whether you can think of positive and negative things at the same time.	
3. What 'impossible things' could you believe?	
4. How could people in your organization be encouraged to think of 'impossible things'?	
5. Suggest a half-hour 'impossible thinking' session every day!	

16

INTRODUCTION

I love talking to visionaries! They have such passion and enthusiasm for their particular field, and that can be highly contagious! But it can also be highly costly – unless you have your feet on the ground. This tale was inspired by an old Aesop fable, and can be used to promote discussion on creative visioning for the future, whilst at the same time considering the more practical and 'down-to-earth' aspects of business planning.

THE TALE

The Creative Astronomer

Every night, the astronomer liked to go outside and observe the stars and the planets in the night sky. Sometimes he would sit on top of a big hill that was near his home, and train his telescope on a particular star. Sometimes he just wandered the streets, marvelling at the beauty of the heavens.

On one particular occasion, as he walked down a country lane with his whole attention focused on the sky, he fell into a deep hole and was trapped. His loud cries eventually brought a neighbour who happened to be passing to the edge of the hole. Having helped him back to safety, the neighbour said, 'You are so curious as to what is hidden in the heavens. How is it that you cannot manage to see what is here on earth?'

MORAL

Look to the heavens – but have your feet on the ground!

Reflections/ Trigger	*Comments/ Thoughts*
1. Are you or is someone you know like the astronomer? In what way?	
2. What is represented by 'the heavens'? Are they too far away?	
3. What is 'the hole' that you are in danger of falling into?	
4. Are people in your organization more 'heaven' or 'earth' related in their approach to change?	
5. How could you encourage people in your organization to be creative and realistic at the same time? Is it possible?	

17

INTRODUCTION

One of the blocks to creativity I meet with regularly (and can recognize in myself) is the fear of taking risk, of having creative ideas but not implementing them. It's a common misperception that there is only risk involved in changing to something new, but in fact there can be an even greater risk in staying still. This story will help you to take up the challenge!

THE TALE

Throwing your Cap

John F Kennedy used to tell this tale of his grandfather, who, as a young boy living in Ireland, would walk past stone walls 10 feet high, whilst on his way to school. The young boy desperately wanted to climb the walls, but was afraid, not knowing whether he could do it, and not knowing what might await him on the other side.

One day, whilst walking home from school, he took his school cap off and threw it over one of the walls. As soon as he had done that, he knew for a certainty that he would now *have* to climb that wall in order to get his cap back, because the punishment he would receive at home if he returned without it far exceeded his fear of climbing the wall!

MORAL

All adventures involve risk.

Reflections/ Trigger	*Comments/ Thoughts*
1. How might this story help you to tackle change more boldly and creatively?	
2. What 'cap' could you metaphorically throw over the wall?	
3. How could you increase in your mind the 'pain' of not changing – for you or others?	
4. How could you increase in your mind the potential 'pleasure' of what you might stand to achieve?	
5. The unknown is only scary because you've never done it – yet! Can you set yourself a deadline for your creative idea?	

18

INTRODUCTION

The famous hypnotherapist Milton Erickson regularly used storytelling as a tool for personal change. He tells this tale to illustrate how we all restrict ourselves severely at times through our limited creative thinking.

THE TALE

Going from Room to Room

I asked a student, 'How do you get from this room into that room?'

He answered, 'First you stand up. Then you take a step…'

I stopped him and said, 'Name all the possible ways you can get from this room into that room.'

He said, 'You can go by running, by walking; you can go by jumping; you can go by hopping, by somersaulting. You can go out that door, go outside the house, come in another door and into the room. Or you could climb out a window if you want to…'

I said, 'If I want to get into that room from this room, I would go out that door, take a taxi to the airport, buy a ticket to Chicago, New York, London, Rome, Athens, Hong Kong, Honolulu, San Francisco, Chicago, Dallas, Phoenix, come back by limousine and go in the back yard and then through the back gate into the back door and into that room. And you thought only of forward movement! You didn't think of going backwards, did you?'

(Extract from *My Voice Will Go With You* edited by Sidney Rosen published by Norton. Used with permission of W W Norton's Company.)

MORAL

We do limit ourselves in our creative thinking. Aim for the moon – and you might hit a star!

Reflections/ Trigger	*Comments/ Thoughts*
1. How does this story change your thoughts about the creativity of change?	
2. In what way have you been thinking too narrowly about a problem or situation?	
3. How could you apply this principle of creative thinking within your organization?	
4. In what situations might you hold 'brainstorming' or MindMapping sessions to generate a large number of ideas?	
5. Discuss what other ways there might be of 'going from room to room'.	

19

INTRODUCTION

My father told me this tale about 40 years ago, and I was never sure whether the story was true or not. I think he must have told me the tale when I was struggling with the rigours of early school days and with the dubious mysteries (to me) of physics, geometry and logarithm tables (what were they for?). It's a credit to my father's storytelling, I suppose, that I can still remember the tale!

THE TALE

A Good Education

Some years ago, a man who had left school without ever having learnt to read or write applied to be a dustman. His lack of formal learning was discovered when he was asked to complete a form for the job and was unable to do so. His application was turned down. Dejected, the man left the council offices.

Desperate to earn some money, and because he had always had a love of nature and gardens, he set up a little market stall in his local village, selling flowers and plants. The business was a big success and he soon had two market stalls and then four and then a great many more throughout the county. Over the years, the man's empire grew and grew, and he even became something of a local celebrity, known for his high energy, enthusiasm and creativity.

One day, one of his employees (of whom there were now quite a number) suggested that he write his business experiences down in a book, so that others could share his ideas; the employee was shocked when he discovered that his employer had never learnt to read or write.

'But just think!' he exclaimed. 'What on earth might you have achieved if you *had* been able to read?'

'That's easy,' replied the man. 'I would have become a dustman.'

MORAL

Creativity doesn't necessarily depend on education or intelligence.

Reflections/ Trigger	*Comments/ Thoughts*
1. What do you understand as the meaning of the story?	
2. Has lack of skill or education ever held you or others back?	
3. Discuss whether creativity can be stifled through 'a good education'.	
4. How could you encourage others in your organization to be creative – even without a particular skill?	
5. Discuss whether you think creativity is linked to intelligence.	

20

INTRODUCTION

This is one of the best-known of the Greek myths, and it serves as a good metaphor to illustrate the dangers that can attach themselves to creativity. There is always a danger of 'flying too high' or 'flying too low' when trying to implement new ideas.

THE TALE

Daedalus and Icarus

Daedalus was born and lived in Athens where he became known as a great inventor and craftsman, having been taught by Athena, the goddess of wisdom and patroness of arts and crafts. Daedalus had high hopes that his son, Icarus, would follow in his footsteps, but the boy showed no sign of intellect or creativity. Instead, Daedalus's nephew, Talos, came to work with him as an apprentice and it soon became clear to Daedalus that Talos, at the age of 12, surpassed even him in ingenuity and craftsmanship. Daedalus grew incredibly jealous of the young boy and saddened that his own son did not have such skill.

One evening, he lured Talos up to the roof of Athena's temple and, pretending to point out certain sights in the distance, caught the boy unawares and pushed him over the edge. He watched Talos fall down and down towards the ground, where he crashed to his death. Daedalus, immediately ashamed of what he had done and fearful of being caught for the murder of the popular boy, took his son, Icarus, and together they escaped to the island of Crete.

They lived there in exile for a number of years, until Daedalus fell out of favour with Minos, the King of Crete. Unable to escape from the island, Daedalus, still the creative inventor, made a pair of wings for himself and one for his son Icarus, taking feathers from the birds and sticking them together with wax from the bees. Having fastened his son's feathers on, he did so with his own and, taking the boy in his arms, warned him, 'Follow me closely, Icarus; do not set your own course. Neither fly too high, lest the sun melt the wax, nor too low, lest the spray from the sea make the feathers too heavy.'

And so, together, Daedalus and Icarus took off from the edge of the cliff and soared into the sky, far away from the island of Crete. But after a short while, Icarus, delighted with his new-found freedom and the power of his wings, soared higher and higher towards the sun.

60

'Look at me, Father!' he called to Daedalus delightedly. 'Look how high I can fly!'

Daedalus turned to look over his shoulder and saw, to his horror, that his predictions had come true and the heat of the sun had melted the wax on Icarus's wings. Powerless to help, he watched his son plunging, just as Talos had done, down and down towards the sea. Icarus crashed into the water, and was killed instantly. Daedalus, distraught with grief, flew down and, scooping up his young son in his arms, carried him to the shore and buried him in the sand.

MORAL

Beware of flying too high or too low.

Reflections/ Trigger	*Comments/ Thoughts*
1. What lessons does the story teach you about creative endeavour?	
2. Daedalus advised, 'Follow me closely; do not set your own course.' Was this good advice?	
3. What creative projects are you involved in where there is a danger of flying too high or too low?	
4. What might be the effect of either action?	
5. How might this story have ended differently?	

CHAPTER 3

Leaders and Teams

'Effective leaders put words to the formless longings and deeply felt needs of others. They tell stories that capture minds and win hearts.'
(Warren Bennis)

The stories here illustrate how sometimes the greatest wisdom is found in simplicity; how we teach people about leadership through our own actions; how leaders and teams can become too dependent on each other; and how reluctant leaders can still make good leaders. We learn how teams who are united can withstand greater attack than individuals; how we can be individuals within a team and still part of a bigger whole; and how all individuals have some inherent worth if they can find their niche. We are warned to consider the image we are creating in our own organization; to beware of the ripple power of stories; and to remain open to the opportunities for learning.

HOW STORIES CAN HELP LEADERS AND TEAMS GOING THROUGH CHANGE

In just the same way that, when I travel on a plane, I watch and listen nervously to the air stewards for the first signs of anything other than *complete* calm and confidence, employees in every area of an organization – particularly during periods of change – watch and listen to their own leaders for confirmation and guidance that 'everything is going to be all right', and as walking, talking embodiments of the organization's values and principles.

In this context, it might be said that the role of modern-day leaders has changed little since those of their forebears – the chiefs, tribal elders or shamans – whose function it was to protect the identity of the tribe, to ensure that its cultural values were preserved and passed down to subsequent generations and to ensure teaching and guidance of the young by providing an aspirational role model. Storytelling was then and still is an integral and implicit part of every leader's job description. (In case you were wondering, these days it's in the small-print section headed 'other duties as required'!) Howard Gardner, in his book *Leading Minds* (1996), says that

> The true impact of a leader depends on the story that he or she relates or embodies, and the reception to that story by the organizational audience.
>
> (Gardner, 1996)

Modern-day leaders, whatever their role or status, can maximize the impact of organizational storytelling in a number of ways:

- by learning to become competent storytellers themselves;
- by having positive stories told *about* them by others;
- by listening and 'tuning in' to others' stories.

Rosabeth Moss Kanter (2002) suggests that the most important personal qualities a leader can bring to a changing organization are 'passion, conviction and confidence in others', and there is probably no better way to demonstrate these qualities than by becoming an organizational storyteller. Such inspirational leadership recognizes and utilizes stories, symbols and metaphors to help people understand the organization's heritage, to paint an exciting vision for the future, to build a sense of team community within possibly disparate sections and to foster a common meaning and purpose. Daniel Goleman (2002), describing the 'emotionally intelligent leader', says

> Leaders have an enormous impact on the overall emotions of an organization, and they are often at the centre of the organization's stories. Managing the myths, the legends, and the symbols of the office can be a powerful driver of change.
>
> (Coleman, 2002)

There is something emotionally uplifting and infectious about listening to someone telling a meaningful story well – the enthusiasm, energy, humour and personal rapport with an audience that are the trademarks of the skilled storyteller excite and engage us far more than listening to someone reading through a business report or a bulleted list.

In the 'story-based' culture that pervades at 3M in Minnesota, they took the bold move some years ago of 'banning the bullets' in their strategic planning process, realizing that

> Bullets allow us to skip the thinking step, genially tricking ourselves into supposing that we have planned when, in fact, we've only listed some good things to do.
>
> (Shaw, Brown and Bromiley, 1998)

They replaced it instead with a process of 'strategic narratives', in which the exponent follows the stages of the traditional story or Story Map (see Chapter 1), ie *setting the scene, defining relationships, introducing the conflict* and *reaching a resolution*, and writes a business narrative around these stages. They found that using a story framework in this way helped both teller and listener to build coherence out of seemingly random information, engaged their emotions and embedded the content far more easily into the memory.

Although there are skills and techniques in storytelling that leaders can learn and develop, not all leaders are going to be talented and natural storytellers – and, even worse than that, there are a number (I think I've met some of them!) who just *think* they are! Does this mean that you can't be a leader unless you're also a great orator? Well, not necessarily. If leaders are at least seen as embodiments of an organization's values and culture through their *actions*, then it can sometimes be left to others to observe and tell the stories about them. Powerful personalities such as Richard Branson, creator of the Virgin brand, Sam Walton, the founder of the giant retailer Wal-Mart, Anita Roddick, the originator of the Body Shop, Sir John Harvey-Jones, one-time Chairman of ICI, and Ricardo Semler, the Brazilian entrepreneur who turned around the fortunes of Semco, are probably as famous for the stories told about them as they are for the results they achieved.

So reflect for a moment on your own organization and ask yourself:

Who are the 'tribal elders' in your organization whom others tell stories about?
What stories are being told about them?
When, where and by whom are the stories told?
Are they positive or negative stories?
Are they consistent with the 'reality' of your organization?
Are they helpful to furthering the aims of the organization?

Are the key values of the organization being passed on through these stories?

How might these stories be captured and utilized more?

Even though the campfires have long since died out, community story-telling still goes on in every organization today, particularly during periods of change, and this process of sharing stories is one that leaders should be aware of and learn to manage. People tell stories for a number of reasons – in order to connect with others, as an emotional release, to share knowledge and experience and to act as a reflective learning tool. McDrury and Alterio say,

> Dialogue that encourages reflection creates spaces in which it is possible to construct meaning... thereby validating experience and opening up the possibility for change. (2002)

Although many of these stories may be lost, some might be captured through the process known as 'learning history', a technique developed by Peter Senge, George Roth, Art Kleiner and others (1999), that draws from the worlds of anthropology, social science, journalism and even theatre. A learning history is a document that tells an organizational story from the perspective of many of the people involved, and is then used as a basis for team discussions. Encouraging individuals to give their personal account of a change event using this format has a number of positive effects. People who previously felt ignored believe that their opinions are valued; it is a chance for people to reflect on their own learning and achievements; it helps to develop trust and confidence, and brings out into the open for constructive discussion issues that may have been 'festering' for years.

The stories in this section can be used by leaders as a tool for their own personal reflection; they can be used to promote discussion as part of a team briefing session, or as a learning tool for coaching, training or development that a leader might employ with a team member. The stories help with these particular aspects of leaders and teams involved in change:

- The greatest wisdom is in simplicity.
- What are your staff learning about leadership through watching others' behaviour?
- Is this the 'lesson' you want them to learn?
- Beware of 'killing your team with kindness'.
- Perhaps there's a leader in all of us.
- United we stand; divided we fall.
- We can be individual and still part of a bigger whole.
- All people have some worth, if they can find their place.
- What image are you creating in your organization?
- Beware the ripple power of stories!
- Learning is all around you – if you're prepared to look for it!

21

INTRODUCTION

Working with a group of senior managers recently and hearing them airing their views (at some length) on the need for 'value-driven behaviour', 'quality plat-forms' and 'competency frameworks' made me think (not that I drifted off at any time, you understand) of the simplicity of Robert Fulghum's advice for leaders given in the following excerpt (1990).

THE TALE

All I Really Need to Know I Learned in Kindergarten

All I really need to know about how to live and what to do and how to be I learned in kindergarten. Wisdom was not at the top of the graduate school mountain, but there in the sand-pile at Sunday School. These are the things I learned:

Share everything; play fair; don't hit people; put things back where you found them; clean up your own mess; don't take things that aren't yours; say sorry when you hurt somebody; wash your hands before you eat; flush; warm cookies and milk are good for you; live a balanced life – learn some and think some and draw and paint and sing and dance and play and work every day some; take a nap every afternoon. When you go out into the world, watch out for traffic, hold hands, and stick together. Be aware of wonder.

MORAL

The greatest wisdom is in simplicity.

Reflections/ Trigger	*Comments/ Thoughts*
1. What wisdom do you learn from the story?	
2. Do you agree with the statement that 'all you need to learn you can do in kindergarten'?	
3. Relate the lessons learnt to your own situation and your own team.	
4. The author suggests we 'hold hands and stick together'. Do you and you rteam do this (not necessarily literally!)?	
5. How could you simplify issues in your own organization?	

22

INTRODUCTION

People very often ask me if the stories I tell are true, and where you might find them. Well, this one definitely is true – and I didn't have to look very far! Many stories are sitting under your nose – you just have to have your own 'story-filter' switched on to see their potential and possible learning points. I think this is an amusing and yet quite sad little story that says a lot about what people learn (sometimes unconsciously) in organizations.

THE TALE

Leadership Games

It's intriguing to observe how behaviour at every level of an organization is very much determined by what is deemed 'acceptable' at higher levels. Some time ago, I was working in a large manufacturing company whose culture was known as predominately autocratic in style. The senior management team made all the decisions for this company. First-line managers, team leaders and operatives of the company were traditionally drip-fed information by senior managers on a strictly 'need to know' basis, and all other information was kept secret.

As part of a workshop I was running on leadership skills, the group of first-line managers had been set a leadership exercise. Their appointed leader for the activity, Anne, had been given the (intentionally vague) instruction to 'sort out a bag of puzzle pieces' within a given period of time. On receiving the instruction, Anne returned pensively to her group, saying, 'I've been told that we've got to sort this bag out. But I don't really know what they want us to do. There's probably a catch to this. We'd better wait and see what happens.' The group agreed with her decision – and sat and did nothing.

Two minutes went by out of the allocated 10 minutes. Anne eventually asked for some clarification of the instruction and, on being told, 'You and your team can decide how you do this', remained just as indecisive. She returned to the group, saying, 'It's still not clear what they expect us to do; I don't think we can make a decision.' And again, perhaps predictably, the group members were happy to go along with her judgement. They sat there for another five minutes – not making a decision and doing absolutely nothing.

I was curious as to what their feedback would be after this activity, particularly in answer to my question of 'Do you think you were successful in your completion of the task?' This group had no hesitation in replying in the affirmative, and went on to explain their rationale, which was that they had acted exactly in accordance with their company 'rules'.

'What are the company rules?' I asked, intrigued, and was very quickly told, 'It's safer to do nothing, rather than make a mistake.'

MORAL

Staff can learn as much about leadership through watching others' behaviour.

Reflections/ Trigger	*Comments/ Thoughts*
1. In what way can you relate to the story?	
2. What leadership styles pervade in your organization? How do you know?	
3. Are people in your organization encouraged to 'do something' or is it better to wait for direction?	
4. Do people in your organization think it safer to 'do nothing' rather than make a mistake?	
5. What might be the consequence of this type of thinking?	

23

INTRODUCTION

I was reminded of this story recently, when I was working with a team of 12 people – but, to be more accurate, it was actually a group of 12 individuals! This story is based on an old Aesop fable. The message is not new – although it's always worth reminding your team that there are dangers in becoming too individualistic, to the detriment of the team. Particularly during periods of change, it's good for a team to stick together (no pun intended!).

THE TALE

The Father and his Sons

A man had a family of sons who, to his dismay, were always arguing amongst themselves. Unable to resolve their differences, the father decided to give them a practical illustration of the dangers of disharmony, and to this end he asked one of the young men to fetch him a bundle of sticks. When the bundle of sticks was brought to him, he passed it round to each of the sons in turn, saying, 'Try your best to break the bundle into pieces.'

As hard as each son tried, none of them could break the wood. Next, the father untied the bundle of sticks and, one by one, passed a single stick to each son, with the same injunction, 'Try your best to break the stick into pieces.'

This time, the task was easy. Each son, with no problem, broke the stick in two. Then the father addressed his sons: 'Let this be a lesson to you; if you are of one mind, like this bundle of sticks, then no external enemy or agent can injure you. But if you are divided and argue amongst yourselves, you will be as easy to break as these sticks.'

MORAL

United we stand; divided we fall.

Reflections/ Trigger	Comments/ Thoughts
1. How can you relate the story to your own experience?	
2. Do teams in your organization see themselves as 'individual sticks' or a 'larger bundle'?	
3. Can some teams be both?	
4. How might this story be used with the team to promote harmony?	
5. What might encourage teams in your organization to 'bundle' together?!	

24

INTRODUCTION

I am indebted to Reg Edwards, who created the idea for this tale during a story-telling workshop run in the North of England in 2001. The team was looking for a metaphor to help encourage a 'reluctant leader' in their organization.

THE TALE

Gregory's Story

Gregory the goose looked out over the lake watching the sun go down at the end of an unusually fine late autumn day. Little was stirring save for an odd hedgehog or two, sniffing out the last of their pre-hibernation feasts of insects and worms. The rest of the geese had already turned in for the night, knowing, as he did, that tomorrow's dawn would see the start of their journey south for the winter.

Gregory had lost count of the number of times he'd made the trip, and had long since forgotten why it was that he simply 'tagged on' at the back. However, he *did* know that, whilst he might not get the praise and recognition of the flight leaders, equally he didn't suffer the pain of such a contribution.

No, Gregory told himself sleepily, he was happy to be a follower. After all, self-esteem and empowerment might be fine for these 'young-uns' but someone like him, with a lifetime of comfort – why change?

Gregory woke suddenly in the semi-gloom, and sensed immediately that something was wrong. He knew he had woken late that morning. He looked out over the lake. A thick, hanging mist lay all about it – the result of yesterday's hot day and quickly cooling night. Within a matter of seconds he realized that he was alone. And then, a familiar sound carried on the still morning air. Gregory recognized the distant sound of geese in flight. Quickly, almost automatically and without fully gathering his thoughts, he launched himself into the air and headed off in the direction of the distant sounds as if being drawn by a magnet.

After only a short time of flying, Gregory felt weariness in his wings; his movements were aggressive and almost panic-like as he fought to maintain momentum against the opposing winds. Oh, how he wished he were with the rest of the geese, tucked nicely in at the back, where long, lazy motions were enough to keep him airborne, taking advantage of the leader's slipstream.

As Gregory flew on, the morning air went strangely quiet – and then suddenly its silence was shattered by two loud bangs. Gregory looked around him in fear, but could see very little because of the mist that still hung in the air. Then the familiar sounds of the geese calling resumed and, in fact, to Gregory's ears seemed louder than before. His heart lifted as he realized that his fellow geese were now much nearer. Maybe his efforts were paying off; his flight must have quickened; perhaps he had worked off the effects of that last bit of pondweed yesterday evening. That could have been the reason why he'd overslept, he thought bitterly.

The sounds seemed to be coming from his right now, but Gregory stayed on course. He knew the route well and settled into his customary flight whilst listening a little more closely to the distant calls rapidly approaching. It was strange, perhaps a trick of the air, but it seemed now as if the sounds were all around him.

Slowly the mist began to clear and, as it did, Gregory saw to his surprise that, rather than seeing a flock of familiar faces, he was actually flying with geese from a neighbouring lake, who were quite clearly distressed and flying round and round in circles. The loud bangs he had heard earlier had been the reverberation of gunshots that had killed their flight leader. As Gregory flew amongst his new companions and became acquainted with them, he realized to his astonishment that, one by one, they were all falling in line behind him. He had become the leader! Panic struck in Gregory's heart.

'What shall I do? Where shall I go? Am I going the right way?' he asked himself.

As if things weren't difficult enough, a strong gust of wind almost brought his forward motion to a stop. But, resolutely, and with a new sense of purpose, Gregory stuck his head down and summoned up even greater effort to fly on, conscious now of the constant honking calls behind him.

Eventually his eyes fell on a lovely heart-shaped copse in the field below. He recognized it instantly, having flown over it many times before. Then looking ahead, he noticed the huge oak tree in the next field and the chimneys of the industrial estate on the horizon. To Gregory's relief he recognized all the landmarks, and realized that he was indeed going in the right direction. The questions he had asked himself moments earlier were forgotten, as he brought the other geese safely in to land...

Gregory took a well-earned drink and thought to himself how strange it was that he couldn't recall the majority of the arduous journey he'd just made – except how very different this journey had been from all the others. One after another, the other geese came up to him to thank him for his guidance – and Gregory glowed with pride. Perhaps there was something to this self-esteem and empowerment 'thing' after all, he thought.

'Who wants to be a follower? Not me!' Gregory told himself.

MORAL

Perhaps there's a leader in all of us.

Reflections/ Trigger	*Comments/ Thoughts*
1. You can be a leader or role model without realizing it. Who in your organization fits this model?	
2. Why is this person a reluctant leader? Is leadership seen as risky?	
3. It's hard at the front, but support from others makes it easier. What support is offered to leaders in your organization?	
4. Some people become leaders when faced with a challenge. How might this be the case in your organization?	
5. Exposure to change can also expose hidden talents. Do you agree?	

25

INTRODUCTION

The inspiration for this story came from a rather thought-provoking entry on the Internet that my sister passed on to me, so it's not clear as to its origins. I liked the principle behind it and how it applied so much to teams working in organizations. It can promote some rather interesting and sometimes contentious discussions.

THE TALE

Harmony

Some are black, some are white, some are brown and some are pink,
Yet they all live together side by side in harmony.

Some are employed most of the time, while others wait patiently for their turn,
Yet they all have equal status in the bigger scheme of things.

Some are downright blunt and one or two are a little on the sharp side,
Yet they all know the role they have to fulfil.

Some are pretty, and some have strange names,
Yet each one is totally unique.

On their own, they can be quite dull and insignificant,
But together they can create a masterpiece.

There's a lot that we can learn
From crayons in a box.

MORAL

We can be an individual and still part of a bigger whole.

Reflections/ Trigger	*Comments/ Thoughts*
1. What lessons can be 'drawn' from the story?!	
2. What is represented by the crayon box in your organization?	
3. What type of 'crayons' do you have in your organization?	
4. Do all the crayons work together harmoniously?	
5. What sort of collective picture are you drawing?	

26

INTRODUCTION

I was recently working with an organization that had gone through a major redundancy programme and, it has to be said, had not handled it particularly sensitively – and then wondered why there was so much unrest amongst the remaining employees! And it reminded me of this Grimm's fairy tale, which I remember being told by my teacher when I was a child – complete with accompanying noises!

THE TALE

The Bremen Town Musicians

A man had a donkey, which he had kept for a number of years. But the donkey was now getting old and his strength had begun to fail. He could no longer carry bales of hay to the market, or carry the master on his back. Secretly the man had planned on shooting the beast, but the old donkey was too clever for that and, overhearing his master's intention, had run away from the farm.

As he trotted down the road, he thought to himself, 'I know what I'll do; I'll go to the town of Bremen and become a town musician. I am sure they could use talent like mine.' And he brayed to himself joyfully as he trotted on, very pleased with his idea. Some miles down the road, he came across an old dog, lying panting and exhausted in the road.

'What's wrong with you, Dog?' asked the donkey. 'Why are you panting?'

'I'm old and tired,' the dog replied. 'Just because I can't run like the other, younger dogs now, my master wanted to kill me. So I ran away. But I don't know what to do now or where to go. What's to become of me?'

'Come with me to Bremen,' said the donkey. 'I'm going to make my fortune as a town musician. You could join me – I'll play the lute and sing and you can play the drums. We'd be a great team!'

The dog agreed and they walked on together. Some miles further down the road, the two came across a cat, sitting in the road looking very sorrowful.

'What's wrong with you, Cat?' asked the donkey. 'Why are you looking so sad?'

'You'd look sad', the cat replied, 'if you knew your neck was on the line. I'm getting old and can't chase mice and rats like I used to. Just because of this, my mistress wants to drown me in the well. So I ran away. But I have nowhere to go now – and no way of finding food', and as if to confirm its anguish the cat let out a loud caterwaul.

'Come with us to Bremen!' the donkey cried. 'Dog and I are going to make our fortunes as musicians. I'm sure you could join in with a fine voice like that.'

The cat agreed and the three of them walked on together. Soon the three passed a farmyard, where the cockerel was sitting on the fence, crowing loudly.

'Good heavens!' said the donkey. 'What a noise! What is ailing you that you're screeching like that?'

'Tomorrow's Sunday', said the cockerel, 'and, because I'm past my best, the farmer's wife is planning on turning me into soup for the family! I'm doomed!' He set up crowing again.

'Don't carry on so,' said the donkey. 'Come and join us; we're all on our way to Bremen to become town musicians. With a powerful voice like that, you'd be an asset to our group!'

The cockerel agreed and they all four set off together. The town of Bremen was too far for them to walk in one day, so when evening arrived they looked for somewhere to shelter for the night. Before long, the cockerel reported that he could see lights in the distance and, on closer inspection, it turned out to be a robbers' den, all lit up, with the robbers sitting round a table laden with food and drink. Between them, the animals hatched a plan for getting into the robbers' cottage.

'Now is the chance for us to try out our musical abilities,' said the donkey.

The donkey put his forefeet up on the window-sill, the dog climbed on his back, the cat climbed up on top of him and the cockerel flew up and perched on the cat's head. On the count of three, they all struck up together – the donkey brayed, the dog barked, the cat screeched and the cockerel crowed. Then with one mighty heave, they all pushed against the window, shattering the glass.

The robbers, on hearing the din, looked out of the window and, seeing the silhouette of a hideous creature with a cockerel's head, a donkey's body, cat's whiskers and dog's tail, thought that a huge giant had descended on them to punish them for their wickedness, and they fled into the woods in great alarm.

The four musicians went into the cottage, and, sitting themselves down at the table, very quickly finished off the food that the robbers had left in such haste. Suddenly tired after their big meal and the great adventure, the four animals chose their place to sleep – the donkey was happy to lie outside the cottage, the dog flopped down behind the door, the cat by the hearth, and the cockerel flew up to the roof.

In the meantime, the robbers were so scared that they never went near the house again, and the four Bremen town musicians were so pleased with their new home that they never wished to leave.

MORAL

All people have some worth, if they can find their place.

Reflections/ Trigger	*Comments/ Thoughts*
1. In what way can you relate to the story?	
2. Who is represented by the donkey, dog, cat and cockerel?	
3. Do they have talents that might be undiscovered?	
4. What 'unlikely' teams might you put together?	
5. What might be the benefit of these teams working together? Might there be a down-side?	

27

INTRODUCTION

Another story inspired by the Internet, so unfortunately I don't know its origins. I have adapted it and re-told it somewhat, so that you can substitute the names of your organization and individuals where you think fit. I have used this story to teach people about the importance of communicating the 'right' image – and this can apply not just when we are recruiting new staff into the organization, but also to communicate to our existing staff during periods of change.

THE TALE

Heaven or Hell?

One day while walking down the street a successful (*Job Title – Director, Manager, Salesperson*) from (*Your Company Name*) was tragically hit by a bus and died. Her (his) soul arrived up in heaven where she was met at the Pearly Gates by St Peter himself.

'Welcome to Heaven,' said St Peter. 'Before you get settled in though, it seems we have a problem. You see, strangely enough, we've never had a (*Job Title*) from your organization make it this far and we're not really sure what to do with you.'

'Can't you just let me in?' asked the woman.

'Well, I'd like to', said St Peter, 'but I have higher orders. What we're going to do is let you have a day in Hell and a day in Heaven and then you can choose whichever one you want to spend an eternity in.'

And with that St Peter put the (*Job Title*) in an elevator and it went down and down and down to Hell. The doors opened and she found herself stepping out on to the putting green of a beautiful golf course. In the distance was a country club and standing in front of her were all her friends – all the other (*Job Title*) from (*Your Company Name*) that she had worked with over the years. They all looked young and glamorous and were dressed in splendid evening dress.

When they saw her, they all ran up and kissed and hugged her and they talked about old times. Later, they played an excellent round of golf and at night went to the country club where she enjoyed an excellent steak and lobster dinner. She met the Devil, who was actually a really nice guy (just a bit misunderstood), and she had a great time telling jokes, singing and dancing. She was having such a good time that, before she knew it, it was time to leave. Everybody shook her hand and waved goodbye as she got on the elevator. The elevator went up and up and up and opened back up at the Pearly Gates where she found St Peter waiting for her.

'Now it's time to spend a day in heaven,' he said.

So she spent the next 24 hours lounging around on clouds with all the other angels. They taught her how to fly, how to sing and play the harp, and fed her the most sumptuous food and drink. Once again, she had a great time and, before she knew it, her 24 hours were up and St Peter came and got her.

'So, you've spent a day in Hell and you've spent a day in Heaven. Now you must choose your eternity,' he said.

The woman paused for a second and then replied, 'Well, I never thought I'd say this, I mean, Heaven has been really great, but I think I had a better time in Hell – and besides, all my friends are there!'

So St Peter escorted her to the elevator and again she went down and down and down back to Hell. But this time, when the doors of the elevator opened she found herself standing in a desolate wasteland covered in garbage and filth. She saw her friends, who were now old and decrepit and dressed in rags, and they were moaning and groaning as they picked up the garbage and put it into sacks. The Devil came up to her and put his arm around the woman.

'I... I... I don't understand,' she stammered. 'Yesterday I was here, and there was a golf course and a country club and we ate lobster and danced and had a great time. Now all I can see is a wasteland of garbage and all my friends look miserable.'

The Devil looked at her and smiled benignly. 'Ah yes,' he said, 'but you must remember... yesterday we were recruiting you... today you're staff.'

MORAL

Beware of the image you are creating in your organization.

Reflections/ Trigger	*Comments/ Thoughts*
1. In what internal/external situations is your organization creating an image?	
2. Is the image accurate? Realistic? Idealistic?	
3. What might be the consequences of painting too rosy a picture?	
4. Can you portray a realistic and optimistic image at the same time?	
5. Do you know how your organization is perceived by others? How might you find out?	

28

INTRODUCTION

I have told this story many times to different groups and individuals and it always seems to resonate with them. I sometimes warn members of management that you cannot actually stop the people in your organization from telling stories – all you can really do is to be aware that this activity is going on, and to be aware of the power of symbolism that some stories carry.

THE TALE

Flying the Flag

Some time ago, a small manufacturing company in the North of England was awarded the prestigious 'Investors in People' award in recognition of its innovative and continuing development of its employees. The company very proudly displayed the plaque on the wall, ordered its new letterhead – and, most importantly to them, flew the IIP flag from the top of a new flagpole, which was placed in the car park alongside the Union Jack and a flag of the company's own logo.

Being in a fairly remote part of the country, the site was prone to high winds and severe weather, and so it was no surprise when one morning, a few months later, staff arrived at the building to find that the precious IIP flag had blown down. What was surprising, however, was the reaction within the organization to this seemingly innocuous event. Within minutes, the news had travelled round the site of the ill-fated flag, and within hours the stories being reported to me were: 'I knew we were going downhill... and now look, we've even lost our IIP award, and the directors haven't got the courage to tell us.'

MORAL

Beware the ripple power of stories!

Reflections/ Trigger	*Comments/ Thoughts*
1. What stories are being told in your organization? Are they symbolic in some way?	
2. Are the stories positive or negative?	
3. Where are they being told – and by whom?	
4. How might this resource be used more effectively?	
5. How can you become a better organizational storyteller?	

29

INTRODUCTION

I very often say to people that stories are all around us – if you have the capacity to hear them. The same, I believe, applies to learning, and particularly during periods of change, when every situation we experience could be a potential learning opportunity. Sometimes we need help to understand the learning – and sometimes we just have to do it for ourselves.

THE TALE

Creative Learning

Socrates, I was reading the other day, described himself as 'a midwife to learning'. He believed that, just like the midwife, his role as a coach was to assist the process along the way – but he drew the line at actually doing the thing for you. He was no more capable, he said, of *making* someone learn, than the midwife was of giving birth to someone else's child.

I was trying a spot of midwifery myself the other day! I had been working with a small group of managers, helping them towards a management development qualification. One these occasions, I often take with me a number of resources to support the learning – books, articles and so on – relevant to the theme of the day, which I arrange on a table in the training room, and encourage participants to browse through any time they have a spare moment. As a group, we hadn't been working together very long, and were still going through the 'storming' phase of our relationship.

On this particular day, David, a newly promoted Client Services Manager, had been the most vociferous in his lamenting: 'How can *they* possibly expect me to do this job?' he moaned. 'If *they* listened to me properly, then *they* would realize what I have to put up with... and', he continued, 'I've never had any training since I joined this company. I don't know how *they* expect me to understand all these procedures...'

On and on he went, citing all the heinous crimes that had been perpetrated against him in his time with the company (none of which had been *his* fault, obviously, but all down to the mysterious and unnamed *'they'* and criticizing the total lack of support and coaching that he had received. I listened and nodded, making the appropriate sympathetic noises, and offered him (hopefully) some constructive comments as to how he might take control and improve the situation. He didn't look convinced.

At lunchtime, the group (including me) went their separate ways, and I was surprised and delighted when I returned to the training room some time later, to find David already there, sitting at the resources table, apparently engrossed in reading. For a moment, as I walked towards him, I felt that warm glow of self-satisfied contentment that midwives must sometimes get, when they imagine that all their efforts have paid off, their advice has been gratefully received and they are about to witness the miracle of birth.

'What are you reading, David?' I enquired enthusiastically as I got nearer to the table.

'Hhmmm?' he looked up dreamily as my enquiry broke him off from his reverie, and folded the newspaper that I could now see sitting in his lap. 'Got to keep up with the football results,' he replied cheerily.

As David went back to his reading, totally oblivious to the books on leadership, learning and motivation that surrounded him, which contained all the answers to the questions he had been posing earlier, and probably much more besides, the warm glow of contentment quickly left my body. This was clearly going to be a long and difficult 'birth'.

MORAL

Learning is all around you – if you're prepared to look for it!

Reflections/ Trigger	*Comments/ Thoughts*
1. What does the story teach you about learning?	
2. Who, in your organization, is or could be a 'midwife to learning', particularly during periods of change?	
3. What learning opportunities are people missing in your organization?	
4. How could you encourage more awareness of learning?	
5. Discuss your last experiential learning situation. Where were you? What did you learn ? How did you learn it?	

30

INTRODUCTION

The inspiration for this re-told story was given to me by a group of trainers from Yorkshire Television at a storytelling workshop I held a couple of years ago. They wanted to deal with an issue of team members becoming too reliant on their manager, and in turn the manager feeling that she was unable to trust them. The wonderful story they created served as a metaphor to deal with the problem in a more creative way.

THE TALE

The Wonderful Wizard

Once upon a time there was a wonderful wizard who lived with a group of elves in the middle of an enchanted forest. The elves loved the old wizard; he was kind and caring; he always listened patiently to their problems and he would create any sort of spell that they asked for – from helping them to find a pot of gold at the end of the rainbow, to getting rid of tiresome dandruff.

But then one day, when they woke up, the elves saw there was a note pinned on the wizard's door, which simply said: *GONE AWAY.* They were bewildered and horrified.

'Where has he gone? How could he leave us? What will we do without him?' were the elves' cries.

Together, they all decided to go out into the forest and look for the wizard. They searched for many days, high and low, even though initially they didn't see too much because they were still weeping bitterly over their loss.

'We'll die!' cried one of the elves, wringing his hands. Another sobbed and said, 'How could the wizard do this to us?'

But then one elf, a little calmer and more confident than the rest, eventually took charge and said, 'Look, we're not going to die. You see those berries on the tree? Well, I've watched the wizard use those in some of his spells. I'm sure they're safe to eat.'

So the elves ate some of the berries and they were indeed delicious. After their meal they started to feel a bit better, so they continued their search to find the wizard, this time looking a little more attentively and positively around the forest.

'Look!' said another, after a time. 'Aren't those the herbs that the wizard makes broth with? Let's gather some and maybe we can work out a way to cook them.'

So, together they started to gather big bunches of the herbs, and eventually they also remembered how the wizard rubbed sticks together to make a fire, and how he added water to the herbs to make the broth. Feeling very proud of their accomplishments, they sat down round the fire and enjoyed their food. By now they were feeling much more cheerful, so much so that they even started to sing: *'Who needs the wizard? We don't need the wizard...'*

In the morning they discussed what they should do, and decided to abandon their search, and set off back to their home in the other part of the forest.

In the meantime, the wizard, who had gone off to visit friends across the valley, started to feel that maybe he had acted a little hastily and, later that day, returned to his house in the enchanted forest.

'I'm sorry I had to dash away like that,' he told his old cat, who was so pleased to see him and was purring happily around his legs, 'but I really needed some space away from the elves for a while, some time to rest, to think and to develop new spells and new ideas. And I have a wonderful new spell.'

He rubbed his hands together excitedly, as he lifted his old spell book and wand from the shelf...

The elves by now had nearly reached their home, and they were still striding out confidently and singing, *'Who needs the wizard? We don't need the wizard'*, when suddenly out in front of them leapt an enormous giant. He stood laughing menacingly and brandishing a club in front of them.

The elves were terrified. *'We need the wizard!'* they screamed, suddenly changing their tune, and then even louder, *'We definitely need the wizard!'*

Although he was engrossed in his spell making, the wizard heard the cries of the elves in the distance, and immediately ran out to see what was happening.

'Oh, wizard!' the elves cried, by now huddling together in a corner. 'Please save us from this giant!'

Now it just so happened that the spell the wizard had been working on was in fact one that he was planning on calling 'The Giant Reducer'™ (patent pending) and he lost no time in trying it out, waving his wand around the giant's feet and muttering the well-rehearsed magic formula. The giant, much to everyone's astonishment and relief, shrank and shrank and shrank until he disappeared with a little puff of smoke into a hole in the ground. The elves were overjoyed, and they hugged the wizard, who was just as delighted to see them, and hugged them back.

'Let's all go home,' he said.

When they reached their own part of the forest again, the first thing the elves did was to build a big statue in the clearing, dedicated to the wonderful wizard and his kindly deeds. Standing back some time later to admire their work, the elves agreed that, as a finishing touch, and to ensure that they would never forget the lessons they had learnt, they would write a meaningful inscription at the base of the statue – and so they did...

MORAL

Beware of 'killing your team with kindness'.

Reflections/ Trigger	Comments/ Thoughts
1. What was the inscription that the elves wrote as a reminder of their lesson?	
2. Who is the wizard in your organization?	
3. Who might be the group of dependent elves?	
4. How might the elves be encouraged to be more self-sufficient?	
5. What might be the benefits of a change in leadership style?	

CHAPTER 4

Dealing with Stress

'If an individual has a calm state of mind, that person's attitudes and views will be calm and tranquil even in the presence of great agitation.'

(Dalai Lama)

The stories in this section help us to identify our priorities in life, and warn us not to allow the problems of the past to carry on into the future. We consider when it is right to persist and when to give up; how to limit the effect of a negative past; and how to be satisfied with what we have and not worried about what we don't have. These stories tell us that too little stress can be as bad as too much; that sometimes 'going with the flow' can be better than putting up a fight; and that happiness is a state of mind that comes from within.

HOW STORIES CAN HELP IN DEALING WITH THE STRESS OF CHANGE

An old trainer's trick when running change workshops used to be to ask participants to fold their arms just as they would do normally – right arm over left or vice versa – and then to reverse the operation, folding their arms the other way. If you're doing this now (and I've done it again to remind myself!), you'll probably realize what a strange sensation it is. People use words like 'uncomfortable', 'awkward' and 'not quite right' to describe their feelings. What we have experienced of course is *change*, albeit a minor one, from what we're used to and feel comfortable with, to something unknown and wholly uncomfortable, together with the accompanying emotions that change can bring about. The trainer, having completed the party trick, could then go on to explain how much more intensified these feelings might be if a person were confronted with major change such as promotion, redundancy, parenthood or moving house.

Anyone who has gone through a significant change in personal or professional life – and that must surely be all of us – will probably report that this was a most stressful and anxious time. And the change itself doesn't have to be necessarily good or bad – or, in fact, *real* – to send us into a stress nosedive. Even imagined change or, to use its technical term, 'worrying' about the 'what ifs' of the future, can produce exactly the same physiological responses we associate with stress – increased heart rate, high blood pressure, breathlessness – and the emotional responses of de-motivation, feeling out of control and low self-esteem.

Story, metaphor and 'story-based' activities can be powerful, yet non-invasive tools in the armoury of dealing with the stress of change, a fact that has been known and used in the therapeutic world for some time and is now increasingly being recognized in organizations. Therapists report that using storytelling – either by listening to clients' 'personal narratives' or by offering them a story or metaphor that might mirror their own problem – affords them the opportunity to 'meet the clients' in their map of the world, and so make progress with them much more quickly.

I recently conducted a one-to-one coaching session with a man who was undergoing some fundamental changes in his role at work, where a large part of our conversation was conducted around a (metaphorical) chess board! He described himself as being the 'pawn in the game', taking small, inconsequential steps and not really having much influence over the whole picture, when what he really wanted to be, he told me, was the knight, 'up there with the senior ranks' as he put it. Continuing with the metaphor, we explored the fact that knights are usually required to fight battles and that, although it was true that they were more senior in terms of their influence, they were also much more at risk of being injured than the lowly pawn. As the metaphor unfolded, we discovered that what my coachee *really* wanted was the kudos and high status of the knight, but with the limited responsibility of the pawn – an unrealistic and dissonant goal, as he eventually agreed, that was causing him a good deal of stress.

Using the metaphor of the chess game, which was instigated by the coachee, gave me an opportunity to understand at a deeper level his feelings and concerns about the forthcoming changes, and provided us with a sort of 'shorthand' and mutually understood language that was a shared experience between us.

People react differently to hearing information in the shape of a story or metaphor rather than just responding to analytical, left-brain-based information. Storytelling is an interactive activity; the listener is not passive, as can be the case when watching television or a video, but is actively involved in the process, using both hemispheres of the brain simultaneously to manage the information – the left hemisphere dealing with content and language, and the right dealing with visualization and pattern recognition. Stories can somehow help us to bypass our normal, analytical functions; we actually become less critical, and more receptive to change and new ideas.

In addition, science has proved that stories can actually help to reduce our stress levels. A researcher at the Pacific Graduate School of Psychology in California carried out tests on the saliva of a number of people while they were listening to stories. He discovered that these people actually experienced a biochemical change whilst listening; their levels of cortisol (the stress hormone) dropped and levels of immunoglobulin A rose. Listening to stories can actually promote relaxation in the listener – a fact that our mothers and fathers must have been aware of when they told us the traditional 'bedtime story'!

And words themselves can act as a powerful sedative. UCLA scientist Dr Lewis Baxter, whilst researching the therapeutic value of language with obsessive-compulsive patients, discovered that listening to well-chosen, spoken narrative could actually activate the same areas of the brain as when a tranquillizing drug was administered. The prescribed drug Prozac causes changes to occur in the caudate nucleus area of the brain, and raises the level of the body's natural sedative, serotonin. Patients hearing some specifically encouraging words experienced the same effect in the caudate nucleus; the narrative actually calmed them down and engendered optimism.

In a business setting, stories and metaphors that are intended to help a person with the management of stress are probably best read privately by the individual and discussed later, possibly as part of a one-to-one coaching or mentoring session, rather than in large group work. It is particularly important, in this context, not to be prescriptive in divulging your interpretation of the meaning or moral; for the story to work, it has to resonate with the listener and his or her map of the world. In his book *The Observing Self*, psychologist Arthur Deikman says,

> You cannot know what goes on in the mind of your client or patient... The client's unconscious, creative imagination will seek and find the "meaning" that is relevant for his or her own situation. No explanation, no direct statement of the story's meaning can substitute for the way it acts on the mind of the hearer.
>
> (Deikman, 1982)

The stories in this section help with these particular aspects of stress:

- Prioritizing what is important in life.
- Not allowing the problems of the past to carry on into the future.
- Managing the stress of communication.
- Knowing when it is right to persist – and when to give up.
- Managing positively people and things from the past.
- Being satisfied with what we have, not worried about what we don't have.
- How too little stress can be as bad as too much.
- How sometimes 'going with the flow' can be better than trying to fight against a certain situation.
- Stress and worry are relative – and happiness is a state of mind that comes from within, not from external stimuli.

31

INTRODUCTION

Modern surveys show that the fastest-growing concern of employees today is lifestyle balance. This first tale appears in many formats, in many different languages; and it's one of the best lessons I know of in time and stress management. It works well as a discussion prompter for helping people to recognize 'time stealers' or as a prelude to a self-review on the identification of priorities.

THE TALE

Filling the Jar

The young man was feeling anxious and troubled about his life and his future, and so one day he decided to take a walk along the beach to try to resolve some of his problems. It was very early in the morning, and the beach was, thankfully, deserted – or so he thought. For as he turned a corner he could see in the distance a strange old man sitting on a rock by the edge of the sea. He had a long, sad face with a white beard and was wearing a silver robe, with a strange pattern on it that the young man had never seen before.

As the young man walked closer, he noticed that the old man was very slowly and meticulously picking up stones and pebbles from the shore. Curious, he walked up to the rock where he was sitting, and, as he did so, the old man raised his head to look at him.

'Why are you so troubled?' said the old man. 'What is the question that you are trying to answer?'

The young man, somewhat taken aback by this pertinent enquiry, replied, almost without thinking, 'I can't seem to work out what's most important in my life. There's so much to do – how do I know what to do first?'

'That's an easy question to answer,' said the old man and, picking up a crude glass jar that had been washed up by the sea, he started to fill it with the rocks, each of them about the size of his fist. When he had filled the jar to the top with rocks, he turned to the young man.

'Is the jar full?'

The young man agreed that it was.

The old man nodded wordlessly, and then picked up a handful of small pebbles and poured them into the jar. He shook the jar lightly and the pebbles effortlessly rolled into the areas between the rocks. He turned again to the young man and this time he smiled.

'*Now* is the jar full?'

The young man smiled back and agreed once more that it was.

Again, without words, the old man reached down and picking up a handful of fine sand poured it into the jar. The sand trickled through all the nooks and crevices left by the pebbles and the rocks. This time there were no spaces left and the jar was completely full.

'Now,' said the old man, 'this is the answer to your question. The rocks represent the most important things in a person's life – whether that be family, partner or children, health, spirituality or wisdom – so that, if you lost everything else and only these were left, your life would still feel full.'

He went on, 'The pebbles represent the other things that matter to you – maybe material things like money, house, clothing or job. The sand', he said, running some of it through his fingers, 'is everything else, the small stuff, the stuff that doesn't really matter.'

As the young man continued to listen, he said, 'Some people make the mistake of putting the sand into the jar first and, if they do – why, of course there is no room left for the pebbles and certainly not the rocks. The same goes for your life. If you spend all your time and energy on little inconsequential things, you will never have room for the things that are really important to you, things that are critical to your happiness. Take care of the rocks first – the things that really matter. Set your priorities. The rest is just sand.'

MORAL

Look after the rocks and the sand will take care of itself.

Reflections/ Trigger	Comments/ Thoughts
1. What lessons does the story teach you?	
2. What constitutes the rocks, the pebbles and the sand in your life?	
3. How will you distinguish between them?	
4. In what order do you 'fill your jar' at the moment?	
5. How might you 'take care of the rocks' more, as the old man suggested?	

32

INTRODUCTION

Psychologists tell us that much of our stress comes from re-living past events, and then worrying about the 'what ifs' of the future. This is a well-known traditional Zen story, which is a powerful illustration of the dangers of habitually carrying our worries and cares with us through life. Like all Zen stories, its beauty and wisdom lie in the very simplicity of the tale.

THE TALE

Carrying the Load

An old monk called Tanzan and his student, Ekido, were walking together down a muddy road. After some time they came to a little stream, and saw standing hesitantly at the water's edge a beautiful young Japanese girl, dressed in a silk kimono and sash.

Tanzan said to the girl, 'Come; let me help you over the water', and without further ado he picked her up and carried her on his back to the other side of the stream. On reaching dry land, he gently set her down again and, having received her thanks, continued on his journey.

His student, Ekido, was furious at such unseemly behaviour by his so-called teacher, and it was much later in the evening before he could bring himself to speak. When he found he could restrain himself no longer, he said to Tanzan, 'Surely you know that we monks are not supposed to have contact with females. What were you thinking of, carrying that young girl on your back across the stream?'

Tanzan smiled at his student's outrage, and said calmly, 'I put the girl down at the edge of the stream. Why are you still carrying her?'

MORAL

The more heavy baggage you are carrying with you, the harder the journey.

Reflections/ Trigger	*Comments/ Thoughts*
1. What do you understand as the meaning of the story?	
2. Can you relate to the behaviour of either of the two main characters?	
3. Are you guilty of carrying 'baggage' with you?	
4. What is represented by 'the girl' or the baggage that you or others might be carrying around?	
5. How might you 'put the baggage down' in order to move on?	

33

INTRODUCTION

During periods of change people become so engrossed in their own 'stuff' that they sometimes forget to communicate – and, with all the sophisticated methods for communication now at our disposal, the procedure should be a simple and carefree one – but is it? Have these methods actually made the process any easier, or have they just changed the rules of the game somewhat, and opened up the field for more misunderstanding, frustration and stress?

THE TALE

Stressful Communication

I'm sure I'm not the only person to receive strange (and sometimes down-right bizarre) telephone messages. We've all pondered for hours over those irritating 'Hello; it's *me*; call me back' directives, whose very brevity can throw us into a dilemma of stressful emotions: there's immediate curiosity to know if we were actually the intended recipient of the message, and then there's the guilt of not wanting to offend the caller by confessing that we have *absolutely no idea* who the caller is, followed by a mild creeping irritation at the 'Well, you should know *me* if nobody else' type of presumption.

Ranking as 'slightly more interesting' on this continuum of communication brainteasers was the message left on my mobile the other day, delivered apparently by an escapee from the cast of a well-known soap opera, whose compelling but economical statement of 'Uh... it's Big Steve; call me la-er, yeah?' was one that left me puzzling for days.

But the contender that gets my vote for the 'most frustrating communication' award must surely be the enigmatic message I received from a male caller earlier this week, spoken in an urgent, breathless and, it has to be said, somewhat alarming manner: 'Hello Margaret... it's Phil... It's **DONE**' (click).

The content of this communication, whose meaning, needless to say, completely escaped me, was particularly disturbing as, first of all, it was obvious that the message was intended for me (or at least someone called Margaret), but, possibly more importantly, I have listed in my telephone book at least four 'Phils', all of whom, I'm sure, would be quite capable of 'doing' the job in question – if only we knew what it was. I started to play around with random possibilities in my mind, and engaged for a moment in a brief fantasy of what one of the Phils (my bank manager) might have 'done', apparently on my behalf. Maybe he'd robbed the bank, or found a way of fiddling my online account to the tune of a couple of million pounds, or perhaps he'd decided to kill off his wife and was ringing to tell me that we were running away together to some remote island...

I came out of this reverie just in time to realize, rather disappointedly, that the 'Phil' in question was, in reality, much more likely to have been my dour, monosyllabic (but very cheap) decorator, ringing to tell me that he'd 'done' the painting in the spare room, and was now inviting me to inspect it.

Coming back to earth with a sorry bump, I mused on how much more effective communication would be if someone, perhaps a government department even, were employed to carry out an 'assumption audit' on every message transmitted between people, with the sole purpose of ensuring understanding between the two parties – but then, what else would we have to worry about?

MORAL

Keep communication simple – and stress free!

Reflections/ Trigger	Comments/ Thoughts
1. Do you find communication stressful? In what situations?	
2. How effective is communication within your organization, particularly during periods of change?	
3 Discuss ways in which it might be improved.	
4. Does modern technology help – or hinder – communication?	
5. How do you know whether your communication has been understood?	

34

INTRODUCTION

Rosabeth Moss Kanter describes the implementation of change as 'a long march', and it's easy sometimes to want to give up on that march, forget all about it and just go home! This story is a simple, humorous reminder to us to keep going, even when we might be on the point of defeat – and I'm sure we've all been at that stage at some time in our lives.

THE TALE

The Two Frogs and the Bucket of Cream

One day, two frogs fell into a bucket of cream. The first frog said to his friend.

'It's no good; we're never going to get out of here', and he closed his eyes and sank to the bottom of the bucket and was drowned.

'We'll see about that,' said the second frog, and he thrashed around in the liquid, trying to stay afloat and swim towards the rim of the bucket.

Soon, the second frog's churning and thrashing turned the cream into butter, and he was able to stand on it and jump out of the pail.

MORAL

If you want to effect change – you have to keep thrashing!

Reflections/ Trigger	*Comments/ Thoughts*
1. Can you relate to either of the two frogs?	
2. Which behaviour is more like you – the 'close your eyes and drown' character or the 'kick up some stink' character?!	
3. Looking back, in what situations have you/others given up too easily?	
4. In what situations could you be more persistent?	
5. What might be the benefits of your persistency?	

35

INTRODUCTION

Paulo Coelho is becoming well known as a modern-day storyteller; his allegorical tales can offer us much wisdom – such as how to set off on the journey of change, and choosing whether or not to make that journey. This story, taken and re-told from The Warrior of Light *(2002), provides an interesting perspective to help us sustain our levels of energy on the way.*

THE TALE

The Warrior of Light

When people ask the warrior of light where he draws his energy from to sustain him on his journey, he tells them that it comes from 'the hidden enemy'. When they ask him for an explanation, and who this enemy might be, he tells them:

'We all have memories of people stored within our minds who have done us some harm in the past. It might be a boy we met at school who fought with us, or a teacher who told us we were stupid. But there is no point carrying these memories around with us, or constantly thinking of revenge, as that only saps our energy. And besides, these people are part of our history, and not part of our story today.

'The warrior of light focuses on improving his own skills, so that eventually his good deeds will be known throughout the world and reach the ears of those who hurt him in the past. Yesterday's pain is the source of the warrior of light's strength.'

MORAL

We can turn past misfortunes to our advantage.

Reflections/ Trigger	*Comments/ Thoughts*
1. What do you understand as the meaning of the story?	
2. How do you relate to it?	
3. Do you have 'hidden enemies'?	
4. Why do you perceive them in this way?	
5. How can you draw energy from these people from the past?	

36

INTRODUCTION

This re-told traditional story by the Brothers Grimm is what is known in story-telling circles as a 'circular' tale. This means that the characters in the story, after much journeying, problem solving and soul searching, end up back where they started – very often a feeling we have when we're in stressful situations. It also introduces the notion of 'why change for change's sake?'

THE TALE

The Fisherman and his Wife

Once there was a poor fisherman who lived with his wife in a little shack down by the seashore. Although *he* was quite content with his lot, his wife seemed to be continually miserable, always lamenting the fact that they were poor, and wishing for a better life.

One bright, sunny day, whilst fishing, the old man was amazed when a large fish he had caught sat in the bottom of his boat, and actually spoke to him.

'Fisherman,' it said, 'please don't kill me. I am actually a Prince, who has had a spell cast upon him. Throw me back into the sea, and I will grant you whatever you wish for.'

The fisherman was a kindly old soul and, without hesitation, agreed to the fish's request. On returning to his home, he told his wife of the adventure.

'You stupid old man!' she cried. 'What are you doing *here*? Get back to the seashore and tell that fish we want a decent house – a pretty cottage would be nice, with roses round the door.'

The old man, rather unwillingly, did as his wife asked and, sure enough, when he returned from his mission, there was his wife sitting at the door of a pretty white cottage, with a garden at the back and roses round the door.

'There now, husband,' she said, beaming, 'isn't this better than living in that awful old shack?'

And so, the wife was happy...for a week or two...and then one day she said to the fisherman,

I've been thinking...this cottage is a bit cramped, and the garden is far too small. Get back to the seashore, and tell that fish we want a bigger house. I want to live in a stone castle, with a big orchard and a lake and fruit trees, and battlements so that people can't see in.

113

Very apprehensively, the old fisherman did as his wife asked, and went back to the seashore where he duly relayed his wife's instructions to the fish. When he returned, he was amazed to see a big castle on the hill, surrounded by gardens and trees and lakes. Standing waving to him from the battlements was his wife, apparently in good spirits, smiling and happy. And she remained happy... for a week or two.

But then one day, she said to her husband,

I've been thinking... it's no fun living in a castle like this. It's draughty and the doors creak and, besides, you can't see over the battlements. Get back to the seashore, and tell that fish we want a palace, the biggest palace in the land, with two enormous thrones so that you and I can be King and Queen. And tell him to fill it with marble and gold fittings, and lush carpets, and crystal chandeliers. And make sure it's got decent heating...

Sadly, the old fisherman went back to the sea and, with a hesitant voice, passed on his wife's demands to the fish. When he returned, sure enough there was a huge white palace, gleaming and shining in the sunshine. It took him a while to find his wife, as she was busily giving out orders to her newly acquired servants. But when he did, he was relieved to see that she was cheerful, and smiling and happy... and she remained so...for a while...

But after another few weeks, the wife, who was sitting on her royal throne, looked just as miserable. She said to the old man,

I'm bored with living in this palace – and bored with being Queen. There's nothing to do, and far too few servants for me to control. Get back to that fish on the seashore, and tell him I want to be Master of the Universe.

'Master of the Universe?' the old fisherman replied, incredulously. 'What on earth makes you ask for that? What would you do if you were Master of the Universe?'

'Well, make a few more decent sunny days for a start,' replied the old woman. 'Now be off with you, and tell that fish what I want.'

With a very heavy heart, the old fisherman went back to the seashore, wondering how he was going to broach his wife's latest request to the fish. But, although he stood in his usual spot and waited and waited for the fish to appear – there was no sign of it.

With an even heavier heart, for he feared his wife's reaction, he returned slowly to give this latest news to his wife. But when he reached the place where the palace had been, he was amazed (and secretly quite pleased) to find that the old shack had returned and his wife was sitting on the doorstep, just as she had been the day he first encountered the fish. From that day to this, he never saw the fish again.

MORAL

Be content with your lot – or you might end up back where you started!

Reflections/ Trigger	*Comments/ Thoughts*
1. How can you relate to the notion of 'going round in circles'?	
2. In what situations have you/ others been dissatisfied with your lot?	
3. How could you learn to be more content with your present situation?	
4. What things are good about your present situation?	
5. What are the dangers of wanting too much?	

37

INTRODUCTION

Working on the current trend in some UK supermarkets of 'Buy one get one free' (or BOGOF as they are delightfully referred to in the trade!), I have included two stories here for the price of one! They share a biological theme, and both raise the interesting and, possibly for some, contentious question of whether we have become too complacent in our lives and don't have enough stress and effort.

THE TALE

Biological Tales

Any keen gardener (of which I am not one, unfortunately) will tell you that young plants need to be watered regularly. However, botanists made a surprising discovery when investigating the effects of too much watering. When young plants get too much rain over a period of time, a short drought can actually kill them. The reason the botanists gave was that, during periods of frequent rain, the plants had no need to push their roots down far into the soil to search for moisture, so they only had a very shallow root system. Consequently, when the water dried up, they had no reserves to draw on and perished very quickly. Over-watering actually made the plants lazy!

Researchers in California some years ago were investigating the conditions in which to grow amoebas. They put a number into two different tanks; in the first tank, the temperature of the water, the humidity, the water levels and other conditions were carefully monitored and constantly adjusted to provide the perfect conditions for growth. In the other tank, the amoebas were subjected to constant changes and exposed to extremes of heat, cold and humidity. To the researchers' surprise, the specimens in the first tank actually died off faster than those subjected to adverse conditions. They concluded that having conditions that are too comfortable actually brings about stagnation and decay, whereas being forced into effort and to adapt to your surroundings promotes growth.

MORAL

We can become stronger in the face of adversity.

Reflections/ Trigger	*Comments/ Thoughts*
1. Do you agree with the message of the stories?	
2. In what ways might you or someone you know be 'too comfortable'?	
3. Are you guilty of 'over-watering' some people in your organization?	
4. In what ways might more effort be introduced – in a positive way?	
5. Is change seen as effort and adversity in your organization?	

38

INTRODUCTION

Much of our stress comes from dissatisfaction with our lives as they currently are, and a constant striving for change and improvement. This is a traditional Buddhist tale that is used to teach about the dangers of dissatisfaction. Hundreds of years ago, Buddhist guru Nagarjuna said, 'Always be content. If you practise contentment, even though you have no wealth you are very rich.' This story is an excerpt from the book Joyful Path of Good Fortune *by Buddhist master Venerable Geshe Kelsang Gyatso (1995).*

THE TALE

The King and the Jewel

Once in India, many years ago, there was a poor man called Telwa who found a precious jewel lying on the ground. He looked at the jewel and, after a while, thought to himself, 'What should I do with this jewel? I am satisfied with all that I have in life. I have no need for it.'

He decided the best course of action was to find someone to give the jewel to, and pondered for a while as to which of his friends and acquaintances had the greatest need. First he thought of all the other poor people he knew, but when he asked them, they all replied that they were quite satisfied and had no real desire for the jewel. Eventually he concluded that the person in most need of this gift was the King.

When he presented the precious gift, the King was astounded and asked, 'Why are you giving this to me, when you are very poor?'

The beggar replied, 'Oh King, you are wealthy and your happiness depends on your continuing to have wealth around you. My happiness comes from a different place and I have no need for this jewel. I therefore offer it to you.'

MORAL

Practise contentment with what you have – don't worry about what you don't have.

Reflections/ Trigger	*Comments/ Thoughts*
1. How does the story relate to your own life?	
2. What is represented by 'the jewel' in your life, ie something you have but don't really need?	
3. Who might you give 'the jewel' to? Why does this person need it more than you?	
4. What areas of your life are you most satisfied with?	
5. Do you agree with Nagarjuna's statement? How easy is it to 'be content'?	

39

INTRODUCTION

Someone said to me, just the other day, while I was, no doubt, stressed out over some minor incident, 'You need to just go with the flow.' 'Hmm,' I thought, 'easier said than done sometimes.' This story is based on an old Aesop fable, and illustrates perfectly, I think, the notion of why 'going with the flow' is sometimes the wisest course of action.

THE TALE

The Oak Tree and the Reeds

Once there was a very large oak tree. It stood strong and unbending in the middle of the field, where it had been standing for hundreds of years. But one day, a ferocious wind blew and blew across the field and, although the oak tree battled hard against it, the wind was too strong, and eventually the oak was uprooted and thrown across the stream at the edge of the field.

As the tree lay dying, it noticed some reeds at the edge of the stream and said to them, 'How is it that I, a strong and sturdy oak, have been defeated by this wind, whereas you reeds, who are light and weak, have survived?'

The reeds replied, gently sighing, 'Oh, oak tree, you are certainly a strong and mighty oak; you have fought and battled with the wind, but in the end you have been destroyed. We reeds bend and twist and move with every breath of air; the wind blows between each of us, and we escape harm.'

MORAL

Going with the flow can sometimes be less stressful than putting up a fight.

Reflections/ Trigger	Comments/ Thoughts
1. What do you understand as the meaning of the story?	
2. Are you generally more like the oak tree or the reeds?	
3. What is the likely result of acting like the oak or the reeds?	
4. In what situations might you or others 'go with the flow' more?	
5. Discuss whether 'going with the flow' is the same as being 'buffeted about'.	

40

INTRODUCTION

One of the suggested strategies of change management is to enhance the perceived pain that people are currently suffering in their present state, in order to increase their motivation for change to a better state. This re-told Nasrudin story is a good illustration of that principle, and yet again raises the question as to whether Nasrudin was stupid, mad, very wise – or perhaps a combination of all three! For more Sufi and Nasrudin tales, see the writer Idries Shah.

THE TALE

Nasrudin and the Source of Happiness

The Mullah Nasrudin came across a young man who was sitting by the side of the road, dolefully picking up handfuls of sand and letting it run through his fingers on to the road again.

'What's wrong with you, my friend?' Nasrudin asked the man. 'You look very downhearted; has something happened to upset you?'

The young man replied,

'No, nothing has happened; that's just the point. I wish something would. I've got a good job, a comfortable home life and I'm in reasonable health. But...', he sighed deeply, 'there must be more to life than this. I want some excitement, something more interesting than I have now. I've taken time out for travelling to try and find some of these things; I want to be happy – before it's too late.'

Nasrudin made no further comment to this lament but, without a word of warning, bent down and picked up the traveller's rucksack and, flinging it over his back, ran off down the road with it as fast as he could. The man, astonished at this sudden and unexpected reaction, got to his feet and chased after Nasrudin, shouting at him and begging him to stop.

Nasrudin knew the area well, better than the young man, and, after several short cuts and diversions, he arrived back at exactly the spot in the road where he had met the unhappy traveller in the first place. He carefully put the bag down, unopened, by the side of the road, and waited in hiding behind a tree for his pursuer to catch him up.

Eventually, the man appeared, and Nasrudin could tell by his face that, having thought he had just been robbed of all his possessions, he was now even more miserable than he had been before! However, as soon as he saw his property lying in the road ahead of him, his whole face changed and he pounced on the bag with great joy, shouting and whooping in the air.

Nasrudin smiled to himself as he observed the scene from his hiding place.

'I'm so pleased to have helped make someone happy today,' he said as he walked away quietly.

MORAL

Happiness is a state of mind.

Reflections/ Trigger	*Comments/ Thoughts*
1. What does the story mean to you?	
2. Do you agree with Nasrudin's method of bringing the young man happiness?	
3. How could you change your own view of happiness?	
4. How might you 'make someone happy' in this way?	
5. Discuss whether happiness is a state of mind.	

CHAPTER 5

Emotional Intelligence

'The brain is just a little box with emotions packed into it.'
(Dr Candace Pert)

This final and very important section in the management of change helps us to develop our own self-awareness and awareness of others; we can consider different perceptions of truth, and understand another person's 'map of the world'. The stories show us how to deal with conflict; how we need to put theory into practice in order to develop our 'emotional competencies'; how to be careful of making wrong 'first impressions' and to 'do as we would be done by'. We are finally reminded of the inherent power in storytelling to generate strong emotions.

HOW STORIES CAN HELP DEVELOP EMOTIONAL INTELLIGENCE

Recently, whilst talking to a chief executive about the need to offer counselling to a number of long-serving employees during a massive downsizing operation, I was amazed when, in the middle of our conversation, he looked at me incredulously and said, 'It's only a *job*; what on *earth* are they getting so upset about?'

Daniel Goleman's (1999) work on emotional intelligence would, I'm sure, have been a revelation to him and many people like him. It introduced us to the notion that it wasn't sufficient for a manager in an organization to be able to read a balance sheet, hire and fire people without breaking the law and have a vague inkling of the difference between 'quality management' and '*total* quality management' (or at least be able to bluff your way out of it!). You were now also required to manage your emotions... unthinkable!

There is sometimes a misunderstanding that the term 'emotional intelligence' requires us to be 'soft and fluffy' or 'nice' in our dealings with others – but this is not the case. Specifically, Goleman's definitions suggest, firstly, that we need to be more aware of our own feelings (*intrapersonal intelligence*) and their effect on our own behaviour, citing such 'emotional competencies' as:

- knowing your own emotions, strengths, limitations and resources;
- being able to control and manage your own emotions, feelings and impulses;
- understanding what motivates you to achieve your goals;

and, secondly, that we are aware of the feelings of others (*interpersonal intelligence*) and how we relate to them constructively; for example:

- being able to understand and relate to others' feelings and perspectives;
- listening to others openly and actively;
- persuading and influencing others positively;
- working with others towards shared goals;
- dealing with conflict and helping to resolve disagreements.

Although one very often witnesses, during periods of change in an organization, the visible behaviours of aggression, hostility or scepticism, the underlying emotions are more likely to be described as fear, anxiety, pessimism and sometimes even despair – and it takes a person astute in identifying these emotions and skilled in the emotional competencies mentioned above to be able to deal with them effectively. For many people, expressing emotions such as these at work, particularly where the culture is described as 'hard' or 'macho', is a taboo area; a display of emotion is perceived as a weakness, a flaw in someone's character.

Expressing our emotions through telling and listening to stories has always been an acceptable and uniquely human characteristic. Indeed, the original purpose of storytelling was to convey, not only facts and information, but also thoughts, ideas and feelings. Part of the original storyteller's role was to explain to the listener the unanswered questions in life – 'How did we get here?', 'When will the world end?', 'What happens after we die?' Parables, myths and legends were created in an attempt to answer some of these questions and bring comfort to the listener. Bruno Bettelheim says of fairy tales:

> Fairy tales intimate that a rewarding, good life is within one's reach despite adversity – but only if one does not shy away from the hazardous struggles without which one can never achieve true identity.   (Bettelheim, 1991)

The original storytellers, unknowingly, had emotional competence in abundance! With no props, visual images and technological gizmos in sight, they still managed to create, simply through their use of verbal and non-verbal communication, a mutual feeling of trust and rapport between themselves and their listeners. As mentioned previously, story-telling is a 'hot', interactive art, and it is this very interaction that creates a bond between the teller and the listener.

Modern-day organizational storytelling requires the same skills – and probably more! For the storyteller who is employing stories as part of a change programme within an organization, the need to know and have rapport with the audience, and be able to appreciate their 'map of the world', is paramount. How do modern storytellers achieve the desired effect?

1. They are acutely aware of their intention in telling the story and what outcome they want to achieve.
2. They have chosen the story carefully, ensuring that it is appropriate and meaningful to the listener.
3. In choosing, they consider such issues as credibility and the culture of the organization.
4. They use language skilfully to create colourful imagery that is both thought-provoking and memorable.
5. They are attuned to the verbal and non-verbal cues of the listener.
6. They match voice tonalities as closely as they can to the audience and know instinctively when to alter their voice or body movements, to bring about the desired reaction.

Listening to a meaningful and well-told story can produce a whole range of emotions – from feelings of curiosity, comfort, elation and laughter, to empathy, sadness, embarrassment and even shock – and it is in this aspect that the real power of story lies. By telling and listening to stories, we enrich ourselves and other people. McDrury and Alterio, working in higher education, say,

> This emotional aspect is one of storytelling's strengths, and perhaps one reason for its recent resurgence, given the call for educators to acknowledge, value and draw on the emotional realities of students' lives.
>
> (McDrury and Alterio, 2002)

When we hear a story – whether modern, traditional, fantasy or fable – its message can lift us, albeit momentarily, out of our own experience, and teach us, sometimes even subconsciously, about other people's maps of the world. From this position, our minds very often transfer the lessons we have learnt about others back to our own situation. If the message of the story resonates with us, we can gain valuable insights into ourselves and our emotions; storytelling can have a powerful transformational effect on us. How many times have you been wallowing in self-pity, and then turned on the television or radio, to hear a story about the latest atrocities from some war-torn part of the world? What happens to your feelings? Certainly, there will be a shift – it might be to sadness, pity, anger or frustration – and, for a moment, your feelings about your own situation are suspended. You may even feel ashamed at your own self-pity.

Telling our own stories can be equally powerful. The process of sharing a story with others can be extremely cathartic; it can provide an emotional release for us, and helps us to make sense of the jumble of emotions in our minds. However, for the process to be effective, it needs to be well managed, as protracted and self-indulgent storytelling will inevitably have a detrimental effect – on both teller and listener!

A technique I find effective, particularly if a person is overwhelmed with negative emotions, is what I call 'third person storytelling'. The individual tells his or her story as though through the eyes of a reporter, and focuses on an imaginary camera. The process helps the person to stand back and take a 'helicopter' view of a difficult situation and, in doing so, encourages the person to separate him- or herself from the emotions.

The stories in this section, which can be used with groups or individuals, are useful for engendering both self-awareness and awareness of others. They help with these particular aspects of emotional intelligence:

● Each person has his or her own perception of the truth – and that may be perceived as something beautiful or ugly.

- Our personal development and growth only come from putting theory into practice.
- Our perceptions are our reality.
- Conflict can become worse if you try to fight with it – sometimes it is better to leave it alone.
- We all need to develop our skill in reading a situation and dealing with it creatively.
- How much time do we spend thinking of ourselves as opposed to the time we spend thinking of others?
- One bad deed has a nasty habit of coming back to haunt you!
- How much do we understand others' 'maps of the world'?
- You can't always rely on your first impressions of a person.
- Do as you would be done by.
- Never underestimate the 'power of storytelling' to generate emotion.

41

INTRODUCTION

I am indebted to Terrence Gargiulo, author of **Making Stories** *(2002), for allowing me to re-tell this story. I think it has that enigmatic quality that we all love in stories, and it's one where there isn't a definitive answer as to its meaning.*

THE TALE

The Search for Truth

Thomas was recognized as a very successful man – he had wealth, fame and fortune – and yet he was still not happy. Whilst trying to analyse his feelings of discontent, he remembered hearing a story as a child about someone searching for Truth, and decided that this must be what was missing from his life. So, one day, he set out in search of Truth. He went to speak with many wise men and women all over the land, gurus, teachers, philosophers and poets, but no-one could answer his question: *what is Truth*?

On and on he went, until, when he was just on the point of giving up, he found himself in a very remote part of the world, and at long last came across a sign in the road, which said 'Truth – This Way'. Overjoyed, Thomas followed the direction that the sign pointed to, and eventually at the top of a hill found a little shack, with a notice outside, which read, 'The Truth Lives Here'. Nervously he knocked at the door, which after a few agonizing moments slowly creaked open; peering out from the gloom was the oldest, most hideous creature he had ever seen, with a hunched back, gnarled fingers and a brown wizened face. In a high-pitched, cack-ling voice she said, 'Yes, dear?'

Thomas, recoiling from the sight of the crone, said hesitantly, 'I'm so sorry. I think I must have come to the wrong place. You see, I was looking for Truth.'

The hag smiled and said, 'Well, you've found me. Won't you come in?'

Thomas reluctantly followed the creature into the little shack and, at her invitation, sat down on a mat by the fire. For many days, Thomas and the old hag sat and talked and discussed and shared ideas, and gradually he began to learn and absorb all the intricacies of Truth. The months turned to years, and Thomas learnt more and more about Truth.

But then one day, he said to the creature, 'Truth, I have learnt so much from you, and I will be grateful to you for the rest of my life. But I feel that now is the time to go home and share this wisdom and knowledge with others, but...' he hesitated.

'What is it, dear?' asked Truth.

'I just don't know where to begin,' said Thomas. 'What should I tell people?'

The hideous old creature leant forward and said, 'Well, dear... tell them I am young and beautiful.'

MORAL

Truth is whatever each person thinks it is – beautiful or ugly.

Reflections/ Trigger	Comments/ Thoughts
1. What wisdom do you learn from the story?	
2. What do you learn about the notion of Truth?	
3. Peter Senge *et al.* (1999) ask the question of organizations: 'How does your culture define Truth?'	
4. Is Truth perceived as the same to all people?	
5. Do people perceive Truth as 'young and beautiful' or is it something else?	

42

INTRODUCTION

We seem to live in an age of complaining; people are so quick to talk about their rights, but not as often about their responsibilities. How often do you hear someone exclaim, 'And do you know, it was completely my fault!' Possibly it's because it's so much easier to apportion blame on to others than to find fault with ourselves. This story is an example of the balance between praising and complaining.

THE TALE

Praise and Complaint

As part of a workshop on advanced coaching skills that I was running with a small group of managers from John Lewis, the retail organization, we got into a lengthy discussion about feedback and the need to achieve a balance between giving praise and giving criticism. This prompted them to share stories about the feedback they received from some of their, shall we say, more 'demanding' customers.

'Why do some people find it so much easier to find negatives in a situation rather than positives? Why do so many people complain but never compliment?' I was asked.

This was a question that I had often pondered on myself, and so I had what I thought was a good answer. I told them that I thought it was because, as customers, if we have a problem, we *have* to complain in order to get the situation resolved. On the other hand, if we have a good experience, there is no compulsion on our part to say anything. It becomes our choice – one that we usually don't take up. A young man in the group agreed and then added another dimension: 'I think it's also because complaining is something we do for ourselves. Praise is something we do for others.'

MORAL

How much time do we spend thinking of ourselves as opposed to the time we spend thinking of others?

Reflections/ Trigger	*Comments/ Thoughts*
1. Do you agree with the concepts in the story?	
2. How can you relate the story to your own experience?	
3. When was the last time you praised someone or gave a compliment?	
4. When was the last time you complained about something or someone?	
5. Discuss how you might achieve a balance between the two.	

43

INTRODUCTION

If you get a chance to read the book The Story Giant *by Brian Patten – do! I bought it last Christmas and had finished it two days later! Brian uses all the magical charms of storytelling – humour, excitement and pathos – with a good deal of wisdom thrown in. This is one of my particular favourites – inspired originally by Aesop – which offers great teaching in how to deal with conflict.*

THE TALE

The Little Monster that Grew and Grew

A soldier returning home alone from a great battle found a monster blocking his path. It wasn't much of a monster. In fact it was quite pathetic. It was small, its claws were blunt, and most of its teeth were missing. The solder had won all the battles he had ever been in and was considered something of a hero. He decided he would deal with the rather feeble-looking monster there and then.

He had run out of bullets, so using his rifle as a club he brought the creature to the ground with a single blow. Then he stepped over it and continued along the path. Within minutes, the monster was in front of him again, only now it looked slightly larger and its teeth and claws were a bit sharper.

Once again he hit the monster, but this time it took several blows to bring it down. Again he stepped over it, and again, a few minutes later, the monster appeared before him, bigger than ever.

The third time, no matter how much he hit the monster it would not go down. It grew larger and more ferocious with each blow the solder aimed at it. Defeated, the soldier fled back down the path, with the monster chasing after him. Yet by the time it arrived at the spot where he'd first seen it, the monster had returned to its original size.

When another traveller appeared on the path the soldier stopped him and warned him of what had happened.

'Maybe we can fight it together,' he suggested, 'then we will overcome it.'

'Let's just leave the feeble little thing where it is,' said the traveller.

'If you pick a quarrel with something unpleasant when you don't really have to, then it simply grows more unpleasant. Let's just leave it alone.'

And so they did. They walked around the toothless little monster and continued unhindered along the path.

(Extract from *The Story Giant* by Brian Patten published by HarperCollins Publishers Ltd. © Brian Patten 2001. Reproduced by permission of the author c/o Rogers, Coleridge & White Ltd, 20 Powis Mews, London W11 1JN.)

MORAL

Don't let your toothless little monsters wind you up!

Reflections/ Trigger	Comments/ Thoughts
1. What 'little monsters' have you had to deal with?	
2. Can you relate to the soldier's experience?	
3. Discuss why the soldier's actions caused the monster to grow.	
4. How do you/others presently handle conflict in your organization?	
5. Is it always the right course of action to 'walk around' conflict?	

44

INTRODUCTION

Recently I was working with a team of senior managers from a financial organization. One of the managers (a particularly vocal character) was convincing me of his obvious wealth of knowledge – he had a long list of MBAs, PhDs and all other letters in between. I made all the right, suitably impressed-type noises whilst listening, and then asked innocently, 'And how do you use all this knowledge?' For a moment, he looked at me as though I had made a rude suggestion, and then said, smiling rather sheepishly, 'Well, I don't use it...' This next story is a reminder of the need to put theory into practice.

THE TALE

The Mantra

There was once a devoted and enthusiastic meditator who, after spending many years studying at a particular monastery, decided that he was ready to share his knowledge and prowess and go out into the world to teach others. Although he was feeling confident that he had little left to learn, his curiosity was aroused when he heard about a famous hermit living nearby, and he felt that he really should go and introduce himself.

The old hermit lived on a remote island in the middle of a large lake, and so the meditator hired a boatman to row him across. The hermit was delighted to have a visitor (he didn't receive many) and together they sat down and shared a pot of tea and some conversation. The meditator, eager to show off his own knowledge and skill, asked the hermit what particular spiritual practice he advocated.

'I don't really have any formal practice,' replied the hermit. 'I just say this mantra that was taught to me.' The old man recited the phrase out loud.

The meditator felt gratified that the hermit used the same mantra as himself, but when the old man said it out loud he was horrified at his pronunciation, and in a rather embarrassed tone said,

I don't quite know how to say this, but, well, that mantra... I'm afraid that's not the right pronunciation; you've been saying it wrong.

'Oh dear,' said the hermit, 'and after all these years. Pray tell me – how should I say it?'

The meditator gave him what he knew to be the correct version, for which the hermit was extremely grateful.

On the way back to the shore, the meditator recounted the tale to the boatman.

'Just fancy,' he said, 'all those wasted years of meditating! What a good job for the old man that I came along when I did. At least he will have some time to make good his mistake before he dies.'

As he got halfway through telling his tale, the meditator realized that the boatman was no longer listening, but seemed instead to be mesmerized by something behind them on the lake. As he turned to see what it was, he felt a gentle tap on his shoulder and, looking round, was astonished to see the hermit, standing on the water beside the boat. The old man smiled at the meditator.

'Please forgive me; I seem to have forgotten that pronunciation already! I wonder if you would mind telling me again?'

MORAL

Our personal development and learning only come from putting theory into practice.

Reflections/ Trigger	*Comments/ Thoughts*
1. How can you relate to the story?	
2. Is there a 'hermit' in your experience that you could learn from?	
3. How might theory/knowledge be put into practice in your organization?	
4. Are you/others guilty of the attitude of the meditator?	
5. How might humility and awareness be encouraged in your organization?	

45

INTRODUCTION

This is a re-told Aesop fable, which illustrates the need to understand and appreciate other people's 'maps of the world'. It can be used to deal with empathy issues, and also the handling of conflict. It can seem so easy, and tempting, to 'get one over' on someone – but invariably action like this will be returned to us – in bucket-loads!

THE TALE

The Fox and the Stork

The fox, pretending to be good friends with the stork, invited her to supper but, when she arrived, all that was on offer for food was a bowl of soup, which the fox served in a very shallow dish. While the fox could of course easily lap this up, the stork could only dip the end of her long bill into the bowl, and so, much to the fox's private amusement, she went away hungry.

The stork, determined to teach the fox a lesson, invited him on a return visit. And so, a few days later, the fox arrived at the stork's home, where a wonderful smell of cooking greeted him. When they sat down at the table, the stork served a delicious meal of fish, but it was contained in a very long-necked glass jar. While the stork with her long bill was able to eat at leisure, the fox could not get his snout into the jar, and all he could do was furiously to lick the outside, hoping to lap up some of the juices.

So the fox left the stork's house, still very hungry, and angry that he had been outwitted.

MORAL

One bad deed has a nasty habit of coming back to haunt you!

Reflections/ Trigger	*Comments/ Thoughts*
1. Who is represented by the fox and by the stork in your organization?	
2. What is the cause of the antagonism between them?	
3. What effect does this behaviour have on others in your organization?	
4. How could the fox and the stork understand each other's needs more?	
5. What might be a different ending to the story?	

46

INTRODUCTION

Daniel Goleman, in his book Working with Emotional Intelligence *(1999), tells us that there is a great divide in competencies between the mind and the heart, or, more scientifically speaking, between cognition and emotion. This following story is a great example of one person's subtle understanding of a potentially difficult situation and also the emotional power of humour and wit.*

THE TALE

Divided Communication

It was Super Bowl Sunday, that most sacrosanct day when most US men are to be found in front of their televisions. A departing flight from New York to Detroit was delayed two hours, and the tension amongst the passengers – almost entirely businessmen – was palpable. When they finally arrived in Detroit, a mysterious glitch with the boarding ramp made the plane stop about a hundred feet from the gate. Frantic about being late, passengers leapt to their feet anyway.

One of the flight attendants went to the intercom. How could she most effectively get everyone to sit down so that the plane could finish taxiing to the gate?

She did *not* announce, in a stern voice, 'Federal regulations require that you be seated before we can move to the gate.'

Instead, she warbled in a singsong tone, suggestive of a playful warning to an adorable small child who has done something naughty but forgivable, 'You're staaaaan – ding!'

At that everyone laughed and sat back down until the plane had finished taxiing to the gate. And, given the circumstances, they got off the plane in a surprisingly good mood.

(Extract from *Working with Emotional Intelligence* by Daniel Coleman published by Bloomsbury. © Daniel Coleman 1998.)

MORAL

Our 'emotional competencies' can help us in reading a situation and dealing with it creatively.

Reflections/ Trigger	*Comments/ Thoughts*
1. What do you think made the flight attendant act in the way she did?	
2. Discuss what other behaviours she might have adopted.	
3. What difficult situations have you had to deal with that required this degree of skill?	
4. Is humour always appropriate in situations like these?	
5. How might you use the learning from this story in your organization?	

47

INTRODUCTION

This is a re-told story of the character Nasrudin, who is also known as the Mullah Nasrudin or Nasreddin Hodja; we met him previously in story 40. Whatever the name, the character has that delightful quality that leaves you pondering as to whether he is really that stupid – or whether there is some inherent wisdom from which we can learn. Traditionally in Middle Eastern countries, Sufi teachers would incorporate such tales as these into the teaching of their students, who would be asked to choose those that they particularly related to and to meditate on them. We could do worse than copy the Sufi teaching style!

THE TALE

Nasrudin and the Falcon

One day, a falcon, blown off its usual course, had landed wearily on Nasrudin's window-sill. Nasrudin, who had never seen a falcon before, looked at it and laughed.

'What sort of a strange bird are you? And how on earth did you get to look like that?'

Not surprisingly, there was no reply from the bird to Nasrudin's questions.

'Well, don't worry,' he said, undeterred at the bird's silence. 'I'm going to help you.'

He set to, and clipped off the bird's long beak, cut its talons short and straight, and trimmed all its feathers.

'There now!' he said in triumph, standing back to admire his handiwork. '*Now* you look more like a bird!'

MORAL

Are we guilty of making others fit into our 'map of the world'?

Reflections/ Trigger	Comments/ Thoughts
1. Discuss the relationship between Nasrudin and the falcon.	
2. Relating to your own experience, who/what is represented by the 'falcon'?	
3. Are you/others guilty of trying to force people into your 'map of the world'?	
4. What problems might be associated with the strategy?	
5. How could you/others learn more about other people's 'maps'?	

48

INTRODUCTION

Many a situation comedy is based on the notion of wrong first impressions, which in turn lead to misunderstandings, mishaps and general mayhem. We can't help making and forming impressions of each other; indeed, our accurate reading of these impressions is an indication of our empathy and social skills. This is a true story of my not-so-accurate reading of a novel situation.

THE TALE

First Impressions

In 2001 Kogan Page published my second book, and I was invited to speak at the American Society for Training and Development's conference in Orlando, Florida. It was only after I got there that I discovered the hotel I had chosen to stay in was created by an ex-Disney designer, but, even if you hadn't known it... I *think* you would have guessed. Looking more like an enchanted castle than a serious place of business, the hotel had walls that were painted pink, and there were turrets and battlements adorning the outside, giving you the impression that, at any moment, Rapunzel might appear and let down her hair from one of the windows.

Inside was just as bizarre; the foyer was decorated not with the traditional potted plants and subdued wallpaper, but with dragons, witches and other fairy-tale paraphernalia. The fantasy theme continued into the bedroom, where the mirrors, bed heads and furniture were taken straight out of a scene from Snow White and the Seven Dwarfs. I thought it was *just* the right place for a storyteller to be! However, a rather more prosaic view was offered by my publisher, Philip Mudd, who, looking round the place for the first time, said, 'Hmmm; I can see why you booked in here. It suits you... it's weird!'

The first morning after my arrival, I went down to the restaurant for some breakfast, curious and rather apprehensive, considering the surreal quality of the place, as to who my fellow 'inmates' might be. At the very least I expected the Pied Piper of Hamelin to show up, or maybe Little Red Hiding Hood might make an appearance! It was worse than I imagined. In front of me, mingling, as I thought, very menacingly, was a large group of men and women, talking together conspiratorially... and every one of them was dressed in black.

While I back-pedalled at the edge of this malevolent crowd, hoping not to be seen, another obvious member of its party approached, and I heard a deep, drawling Texan voice say, 'Can I step in front of you?'

I swear the man was 7 feet tall, dressed in the obligatory black, with a long ponytail hanging down his back, and thick metallic chains clanking around his neck, wrist and belt. I didn't think this was an appropriate time to state my rights and explain that I had been waiting in the queue longer than him.

'Fine! Of course! Why not?' I heard my own voice reply, in a nervous (and very British) squeak. To my amazement, the man struck up a conversation, and, emboldened (but not deceived) by his apparent normality, I gestured to the other members of the crowd, and asked, still rather tremulously, 'Are you... all here together?'

'Yeah,' said the man, in the same slow drawl. 'We're part of a group. We meet once a year.'

This additional information did nothing to allay my growing fears. What sort of strange convention had I wandered into? My mind started to drift – scenes of the Mafia, drug dealing and ritual killings were by now filling my overripe imagination.

'And... uhhh... what do you and your group actually... uhh... do?' I asked, not sure if I really wanted to know the answer.

The giant looked down at me and then very slowly replied, 'We're... all... hairdressers.'

MORAL

First impressions can be misleading!

Reflections/ Trigger	Comments/ Thoughts
1. What cautionary lessons do you learn from the story?!	
2. What situations have you experienced where you formed an erroneous first impression?	
3. What are the first impressions based on?	
4. What might be the result of a 'wrong' first impression?	
5. Can we avoid having a first impression? Is it wrong to do this?	

49

INTRODUCTION

It's easy when we're young to look with contempt at the frail or elderly, thinking ourselves exempt and immune from such a future. But sadly, it comes to us all, and this re-told Grimm story is a poignant reminder of that fact, and the need for us to show empathy to those less fortunate than ourselves.

THE TALE

The Old Man and his Grandson

There was once a very old man, who lived with his son, daughter-in-law and small grandson. He was so old that his hands trembled constantly, his back was bowed and his eyes were dim with age. When he sat down at the dining table to eat, his hands shook so much that they could hardly hold a spoon, and very often he would spill soup on the daughter-in-law's clean tablecloth.

'For goodness' sake!' the young wife would exclaim. 'Can't you tell your father to eat properly? I can't stand him at the table with us any longer.' And she and her husband made the old man sit in a corner by the stove out of sight from the rest of the family.

They put his food into a very rough earthenware bowl, which the old man could barely hold. One day, his hands shook so much that the whole thing went crashing to the ground. The young wife was furious, and again said to her husband,

'Can't you do something with your father? He's a disgrace to the family.'

This time they bought him a rough wooden bowl, and fed him hardly anything at all, so that the old man got weaker and weaker.

His little grandson, who was just four years old, had been observing all this and, one day, his parents saw him gathering bits of wood and piling them into a corner of the room.

'What are you doing, son?' asked his father.

'I am making two little bowls, just like the one you gave grandfather,' the child replied sagely, 'so that you and Mother can eat out of them when I am bigger.'

The husband and his wife looked at each other and then at the old man, and slowly both their faces became awash with tears. Silently they helped the old man back to the table, and never scolded him again when he spilt his food.

MORAL

Do as you would be done by.

Reflections/ Trigger	*Comments/ Thoughts*
1. What does the story teach you?	
2. Why do you think the husband and wife were reacting as they did?	
3. Who is represented by the old, frail man for you?	
4. How are more mature employees treated in your organization?	
5. We talk about 'knowing what it's like to be in someone's shoes' – but do we really know? Discuss your views.	

50

INTRODUCTION

The power of storytelling lies in its ability to generate strong emotions – positive and negative. I hope that this final story leaves you with the inspiration to find ways of utilizing that power within your own organization.

THE TALE

The Power of Storytelling

It was only two weeks since the horrors of 11 September 2001, and I was scheduled to run a workshop in London entitled 'The Power of Storytelling'. There was a good mix of participants on the course, made up of managers, trainers and consultants, and we had had a very enjoyable and productive day. I normally end these workshops with a special story, and like to choose one that I think will resonate with the listeners and leave them with something to ponder.

The destruction of the twin towers had had a profound effect on me, as with so many others. I feel a certain affinity with the United States, having worked there on a number of occasions, and I have both friends and colleagues there. The story I had chosen to tell, which I thought was most appropriate to the current situation, was the US humorist James Thurber's 'The Last Flower', written in 1939. It's an allegorical story, which tells in Thurber's inimitable quirky yet powerful way of the poignancy, futility and almost inevitability of war and conflict.

I finished reading the tale, and for a moment there was that magical silence that often comes at the end of such a storytelling. I looked up and realized that there was not one person in the room (male or female) whose eyes weren't full of tears. My first reaction was one of concern. Should I have told that story? Had I depressed everyone at the end of the day? But then, just when I was on the point of apologizing, I remembered the title of my workshop, 'The Power of Storytelling' – this surely was the best illustration I could have given them.

MORAL

Never underestimate the 'power of storytelling'.

Reflections/ Trigger	*Comments/ Thoughts*
1. What stories have you heard that have provoked some emotion in you?	
2. What stories do you remember most?	
3. 'Storytelling enriches ourselves and other people.' Do you agree?	
4. How might you incorporate storytelling more into your organization?	
5. How might you incorporate positive emotions – curiosity, humour, excitement – into your organization?	

References and Further Reading

Bennis, W (1996) The leader as storyteller, *Harvard Business Review*, Jan/Feb, **74** (1), pp 154–61

Bettelheim, B (1991) *The Uses of Enchantment: The meaning and importance of fairy tales*, Penguin, London

Boden, M (1996) *The Creative Mind*, Abacus, London

Bridges, W (1999) *Managing Transitions*, Nicholas Brealey, London

Buzan, T (1993) *The Mind Map Book*, BBC Books, London

Campbell, J (1993) *The Hero with a Thousand Faces*, Fontana Press, London

Coelho, P (2002) *The Warrior of Light*, HarperCollins, New York

Deikman, A (1982) *The Observing Self*, Beacon Press, Boston, MA

Denning, S (2001) *The Springboard: How storytelling ignites action in knowledge-era organizations*, Butterworth-Heinemann, New York

Drucker Foundation (2002) *On Leading Change*, Jossey-Bass, San Francisco

Fulghum, R (1990) *All I Really Need to Know I Learned in Kindergarten*, HarperCollins, New York

Gardner, H (1996) *Leading Minds: An anatomy of leadership*, Basic Books, New York

Gargiulo, T (2002) *Making Stories: A Practical Guide for Organizational Leaders and Human Resource Specialists*, Quorum Books, Westport, CT

Goleman, D (1999) *Working with Emotional Intelligence*, Bloomsbury, London

Goleman, D (2002) *The New Leaders*, Little, Brown, London

Gyatso, G (1995) *Joyful Path of Good Fortune*, Tharpa Publications, UK

Handy, C (2002) *The Elephant and the Flea*, Hutchinson, London

Hart, L (1975) *How the Brain Works: A new understanding of human learning*, Basic Books, New York

Jensen, E (1995) *The Learning Brain*, Turning Point Press, San Diego, CA

Lackoff, G and Johnson, M (1980) *Metaphors We Live By*, University of Chicago Press, Chicago

Lawley, J and Tompkins, P (2000) *Metaphors in Mind*, Developing Company Press, London

Lozanov, G (1978) *Suggestology and Outlines of Suggestopedy*, Gordon & Breach, New York

McDrury, J and Alterio, M (2002) *Learning through Storytelling in Higher Education*, Kogan Page, London

Mellon, N (1992) *Storytelling and the Art of Imagination*, Element Books, Shaftesbury

Mitroff, L and Kilmann, R H (1975) Stories managers tell: a new tool for organizational problem solving, *Management Review*, July, pp 18–28

Morgan, G (1997) *Images of Organization*, Sage, Thousand Oaks, CA

Neuhauser, P (1993) *Corporate Legends and Lore*, McGraw-Hill, New York

O'Keefe, J and Nadel, L (1978) *The Hippocampus as a Cognitive Map*, Clarendon Press, Oxford

Parkin, M (1998) *Tales for Trainers*, Kogan Page, London

Parkin, M (2001) *Tales for Coaching*, Kogan Page, London

Rosen, S (1982) *My Voice Will Go with You*, WW Norton, New York

Senge, P *et al* (1999) *The Dance of Change*, Nicholas Brealey, London

Shaw, G, Brown, R and Bromiley, P (1998) Strategic stories: how 3M is rewriting business planning, *Harvard Business Review*, May–June

Von Oech, R (1998) *A Whack on the Side of the Head*, Warner Books, New York

Further Information

If you would like to learn more about using storytelling to develop people and organizations for example:

- enhancing your presentation skills using stories and metaphors;
- incorporating a 'story-based' culture in your organization;
- making learning easier and longer lasting;

contact Margaret Parkin at Training Options (e-mail: training_options@ tiscali.co.uk; Web site: www.trainingoptionsuk.com). *Free* monthly newsletter containing stories and tips on storytelling!

Index

Also by Margaret Parkin:

Tales for Trainers
Using Stories and Metaphors to Facilitate Learning

Margaret Parkin's guide to using stories, anecdotes, metaphors and poetry in training and development is packed with ideas to give training more impact. Beginning by setting the use of stories in learning on a sound theoretical footing, the book goes on to include sample stories that trainers can read aloud. Echoing the successful story-based approach of *Chicken Soup for the Soul*, etc, the author provides 50 tales that will immediately help trainers, managers, educators and coaches to reinforce key messages or stimulate fresh thinking. Proven to work in a variety of training environments the stories themselves range from ones written specifically by the author to carefully selected extracts from literature (everything from Lewis Carroll to James Thurber). The linking factor in all of the stories is that they each work brilliantly as an aide to learning.

Tales for Coaching
Using Stories and Metaphors with Individuals & Small Groups

Showing you how and when to use stories to maximum effect, whether you are coaching an individual or a group, the book demonstrates how your coaching can have greater impact with the effective use of storytelling. Complete with sample stories that can be used in a variety of coaching situations, *Tales for Coaching* includes 50 tales that will immediately help coaches, trainers, managers and educators to reinforce key messages to stimulate fresh thinking. The stories themselves range from those written specifically by the author to carefully selected material from literature (everything from Aesop and Winnie the Pooh to Stephen Covey). Each tried and tested tale is a proven and effective aid to improve coaching.

Both the above titles are available from all good bookshops. To obtain further information, please contact the publisher at the address below:

Kogan Page Limited
120 Pentonville Road
London N1 9JN
Tel: 020 7278 0433
Fax: 020 7837 6348
www.kogan-page.co.uk